The Kingdom Promise:
How Leading Canadians Choose Faith to Conquer the Storms of Life

"But seek ye first the kingdom of God and his righteousness; and all these things shall be added unto you."
Matthew 6:33 KJV

THE Kingdom PROMISE

HOW LEADING CANADIANS CHOOSE FAITH TO CONQUER THE STORMS OF LIFE

GARY GRADLEY AND PHIL KERSHAW

CASTLE QUAY BOOKS

The Kingdom Promise: How Leading Canadians Choose Faith to Conquer the Storms of Life

Printed in Canada
International Standard Book Number: 978-1-894860-32-1
ISBN 978-1-894860-25-3 EPUB

Published by:
Castle Quay Books
Pickering, Ontario
Tel: (416) 573-3249
E-mail: info@castlequaybooks.com   www.castlequaybooks.com

Edited by Marina Hofman-Willard and Lori MacKay
Cover design by Burst Impressions
Printed at Essence Printing, Belleville, Ontario

Scripture quotations marked KJV are from The Holy Bible, King James Version. Copyright © 1977, 1984, Thomas Nelson Inc., Publishers. All rights reserved. Scripture quotations marked NKJV are taken from the New King James Version. Copyright © 1979, 1980, 1982. Thomas Nelson Inc., Publishers.

Library and Archives Canada Cataloguing in Publication

Gradley, Gary, 1957-

The kingdom promise : how leading Canadians choose faith to conquer the storms of life / Gary Gradley and Phil Kershaw.

Issued also in electronic format.

ISBN 978-1-894860-32-1

1. Christian life--Canada. 2. Faith. I. Kershaw, Phil, 1948- II. Title.

BV4501.3.G67 2012   248.8'6   C2012-906049-6

CASTLE QUAY BOOKS

Thanks

Individuals who took the time to be interviewed and share their stories of walking in faith: Agnes Fraser, Andy and Judy Atkins, Annmarie Morais, Bill Sanger, Bob Lucas, Bruce Smith, Bruxy Cavey, Chito Ramos, David Mainse, Don Cherry, Don Simmonds, Don Vialoux, Donna Messer, Frank Buchanan, Gary Gregor, Gerry O'Mahoney, Glenn Mowat, Gordon R. (anonymous), Godfrey Chisholm, Henry Verrier, Bryan Freeman and Joel Auge, Jamie Demarchi, Jan Eden, Jeff Russo, Jim Mueller, Jill W. (anonymous), John Arnott, John and Eloise Bergen, Keith Pelly, Ken and Ruth Copsey, Lorna Dueck, Marguerite Zimmerman, Mark Potter, Mel Stevens, Mike Gartner, Myles Munroe, Neleitha Hewitt, Paul Henderson, Phil Geldart, Philip Phillips, Ron Ellis, Rose Clark, Thomas Henshell, Tim Cestnick, Tom Schmidt and Winsome Johnson.

Contents

Acknowledgements

This entire book-writing process has been an incredible walk in faith. So first I humbly thank God for enabling, facilitating, harmoniously resourcing and provisioning the writing, funding and publishing of this book. I thank God for Bruce Smith, who really accelerated my vision and belief in this book and introduced me to Phil Kershaw, my co-author.

I am endlessly grateful for Phil's absolute commitment of hundreds of hours of writing time, for his intellect and business experience, for his intuitive wisdom, for his spiritual authenticity and his wonderful communication skills.

I enjoyed and appreciated the 45 individuals that I interviewed for the book. They were an inspiration that dramatically raised my faith by seeing them walk by faith through some of the most difficult of life's challenges. Unfortunately we couldn't include all 45 of them, but all of their stories were worthy.

I honour with great appreciation our financial supporters who made possible the publishing of this book. Without them you would not be reading this book now. They are generous believers committed to building the kingdom of God. I thank them deeply.

And to my faithful prayer supporters who have encouraged me through prayer through many challenges over the years, I am thankful.

We appreciated the incredible service, wisdom and advice from our publisher, Larry Willard of Castle Quay Books, and his capable staff. He was always there to help and advise.

I am grateful for my loving family, my wife, Lori, and my teenage children, Kevin and Shauna, for their years of patience and acceptance of my long work hours and busy schedule.

And most of all I am forever grateful to God, Jesus Christ and the Holy Spirit for peace, guidance, provision and saving my life! Thank you.

For his purpose and glory!

With gratitude and blessings,
Gary Gradley

First I want to thank God and Jesus; without their forgiveness and grace I wouldn't even be here today.

Secondly I want to thank pastors Bruce Smith and Neleitha Hewitt, who mentored and encouraged me in matters of the Spirit and the Bible that brought me to the revelations of the Scripture revealed within.

I want to recognize Gary Gradley for his inspiration to create a book of testimonials of faith and his labour in acquiring and documenting these, and of course our incredible publisher, Larry Willard, for seeing this vision and having the commitment to allow us to bring it to life.

On a personal note I want to recognize my friend Linda Bradshaw for her support, encouragement and correction, which were necessary to complete this task.

Finally I want to thank my family, my three children, Kris, Mike and Vel, and my grandchildren, spread out across North America, who always inspire me and make me grateful for every day.

God bless,
Phil Kershaw

Introduction

Gary Gradley

One cold, dark, depressing day in February 2009 I woke up in a state of fear and depression. I realized that I was in a lot of trouble financially. I had $50,000 in personal credit card debt and was over-leveraged in my rental real estate mortgages. Perhaps you can relate to these overwhelming feelings of fear and hopelessness, believing that there is no way out of a deep financial hole. Perhaps you know someone who is in a similar situation.

I went to a place of fear, depression and hopelessness, a bad place to be. I would never wish this kind of financial stress and emotional pain on anyone. I had been choosing and believing in financial lack and limitation, and I was filled with a tremendous amount of doubt and fear and cynicism.

One day, after feeling hopeless for three months, I came to a place where I was sick and tired of feeling hopeless. I decided then and there that I would never feel that hopeless ever again. Hopelessness is a silent and deadly killer. When we lose our hope and faith we are as good as dead.

That was an important shifting point for me. I finally realized what I had been doing to myself: creating a self-fulfilling fear-based prophecy of more financial lack and limitation.

Because of my own failure, I wanted and needed to learn what successful people were dong that I wasn't doing. How did they think? What did they believe? How did they become successful? What state of being were they in (doubt vs. faith)? What was their relationship with God? Was that connected to their success? What did they trust in? I decided to start interviewing successful people to learn what I could do differently to improve my lifestyle.

I discovered that for all of them, their faith played a critical role in their success. Most people said that their faith in God was the foundation and cause of their success. Especially during life's most challenging times, their faith in God brought them through the crises. I was able to capture the emotion and faith of their stories as they walked through many difficult trials and tribulations of financial loss, bankruptcy, major health issues, life-threatening diseases, relationship issues, divorce and the death of loved ones, especially children.

Their faith enabled them to conquer their storms in life.

At about the same time, I felt called to make a career change and pursue a new role as a fundraiser for a Christian humanitarian organization in Canada. I felt strongly in my heart that it was the right move for me, even though there were lots of challenges, especially income-wise.

In this new fundraising role, I had no other choice except to walk by faith: faith that God would provide the donors and provide for my financial needs.

So as I was now experiencing what it was like to walk by faith and had interviewed 45 different people, I felt called to gather all this information together and put it in a book for others to benefit from.

For me, the collection of all these true stories of faith has provided overwhelming evidence of the unlimited power of faith and of God, which has dramatically raised my faith. I now know that when we seek God and all his righteousness through deep daily devotion, prayer and righteous living, all these things will be added unto us.

God's promise has been fulfilled in my life, as God has harmoniously provided a full-time fundraising job, an insurance claim payout of $28,000 and the sale of two of our rental properties, which has significantly reduced our debt.

At the time of printing this book I have paid off the $50,000 in credit card debt through faith, God's provision, spending discipline and monthly payments. What a difficult "pay-off debt" journey it has been, with the life lesson of never going into debt again! Debt is a stressful killer.

Thank God (literally) that my finances have dramatically improved! The fundamental difference was my faith. The dramatic raising of my faith in God was the primary thing that really changed. The transformation started when I consistently chose faith over fear.

My other big lesson was that every moment we choose in our thoughts and emotions either fear or faith. We have the power of free choice, and

I believe that it is our responsibility to choose our thoughts and emotions, choose our state of being.

I believe we must develop our mental-emotional strength to use our power of choice to consciously live and walk in a state of love. We must choose every moment to love everything, just like Jesus did. Jesus is our role model for right living and the best example of the power of love.

To love everything means to accept, not resist; to love unconditionally, not judge and despise; and to totally trust that life is unfolding perfectly as it should. When we do this, we experience peace!

So don't focus on and worry about the economy. Instead focus on your own state and soul. Decide to manage your inner world of thoughts and emotions first as the top priority.

Decide to choose faith over fear by totally trusting God. When we trust God, we can more easily choose love every moment. When we choose love, since God is love we become one with God.

Rely 100 per cent on God. To conquer the oncoming storms of life personally and globally, we must totally trust God and choose love and faith over fear every moment.

Based on my personal experience and the overwhelming evidence of God's provision, I've come to the firm conclusion that faith in God is the only real solution, especially in times of chaos and crisis. I now know that when we have full faith and no doubt and totally trust in God, God will provide perfectly for all our needs.

This was the impetus for writing this series of books under the banner of *Trusting Through the Transition*.

The first installment of this series, which you now have, is co-authored by Phil Kershaw and entitled *The Kingdom Promise: How Leading Canadians Choose Faith to Conquer the Storms of Life*.

We hope that you find it an enjoyable and inspiring read, that it moves your heart and builds your faith.

The second book in the series is *Conquering the Social Economic Storm: Your Practical Personal and Financial Survival Guide to Thriving through the Transition*.

This book and workshop combine and integrate the important elements of spiritual, mental and emotional practices with sound financial principles and practices to prepare you and your family to survive and thrive through the transition. See the back of the book for more details and our resource and contact information.

In concluding I wanted to share my personal and ministry vision and mission so you will understand my purpose and intent.

Vision: Seeing humanity live on purpose for God, together in love, faith, harmony and peace.

Mission: To serve God by expanding the kingdom of God through presenting spiritual and practical truths, guidance, leadership and methods to inspire, encourage and transform millions of people's lives. To accelerate faith by providing overwhelming evidence and proving God's fulfillment and provision of Matthew 6:33: *"But seek ye first the kingdom of God, and his righteousness; and all these things shall be added unto you"* (KJV).

To support people in walking righteously in faith and to prepare them mentally, emotionally, physically, financially and spiritually to lead through any spiritual and social-economic crisis relatively unscathed.

To save 100,000 lives: this would target 100,000 of the poorest people in the world through charitable giving and service.

I encourage you to deliberately build your faith and your trust now! I encourage you to daily *"Seek ye first the kingdom of God, and his righteousness; and all these things shall be added unto you"* (Matthew 6:33 KJV).

Please take and use what we have provided in this book so that you can rely on the Kingdom Promise and choose faith over fear in conquering the storms of life.

For his purpose and glory!

With gratitude and blessings,
Gary Gradley

CHAPTER 1

The Promises of God

"The LORD is trustworthy in all he promises and faithful in all he does."

Psalm 145:13 NIV

The Kingdom Promise is based on Scripture from the book of Matthew. It speaks to what God has promised us when we enter into a covenant relationship with him.

The purpose of this book is to give you the tools to build your faith, by two means:

One: Presenting the biblical principles and Scriptures that deal directly with God's faithfulness. In so doing we will endeavour to build on your understanding and appreciation of these principles and Scriptures.

Two: Providing overwhelming evidence by a series of testimonials from Canadians, both well-known, like Dr. David Mainse, Lorna Dueck, Paul Henderson and Don Cherry, and not so well-known, who have amazing testimonies of faith and overcoming horrendous obstacles and triumphing.

My belief is that by doing this the book can be an invaluable tool for believers to strengthen their faith and also a great evangelical tool to reach out to non-believers so that, as they say, "When you've tried everything else, try Jesus."

This book is entitled *The Kingdom Promise* because it speaks to the principles and covenants that God has offered us. There are 1,260 promises in the Bible, which is why this book is so significant to our lives.

The Kingdom Promise

The *Oxford Dictionary* defines *promise* as "a declaration or assurance that one will do something or that a particular thing will happen." In fact there is no stronger commitment than a promise that can be made. However, as we all know, a promise is only as good as the authority, credibility and intention of whoever is making it.

Therefore, as there is no higher authority than God himself and there is no higher commitment than a promise, we need to study and understand this.

These promises are revealed through what is referred to in the Bible as a covenant. A biblical covenant is an agreement between God and his people in which God makes certain promises. It is unconditional, whereas a contract is conditional and based on agreed upon guidelines.

Specifically, God formed a covenant with Abraham in which he blessed his seed for eternity: *"Blessing I will bless you, and multiplying I will multiply your descendants as the stars of the heaven"* (Genesis 22:17 NKJV).

Now this is significant to us as Christians as we are grafted into this covenant through the blood of Jesus, as was revealed by the apostle Paul in the New Testament: *"That the blessing of Abraham might come upon the Gentiles in Christ Jesus, that we might receive the promise of the Spirit through faith"* (Galatians 3:14 NKJV).

This is important because as we face our crises and fears, we are going to be looking for "evidence" that God has both made and fulfilled his promises over the ages to his descendants who are operating under Abraham's covenant.

This is key, because it states unilaterally that we as believers of Jesus are blessed, as are our descendants. This then forms the basis of our faith, which is to believe and trust in that blessing and that its benefits will flow to us.

In this book you will see modern-day examples of Canadians just like you and me who have been the recipient of this blessing and are now sharing their testimonies. We have attempted to cast as wide a net as possible, stretching from pastors such as Dr. David Mainse and Bruxy Cavey to sports icons like Don Cherry, Paul Henderson and Ron Ellis.

We have attempted on purpose to uncover aspects of their lives that are not well known, as a means of revealing the total people behind the public personae as they disclose intensely personal and sometimes difficult circumstances in their lives.

Other people in the book will probably not be known to you. They range from missionaries serving in Africa to recent immigrants to Canada who share their trials and how faith pulled them through seemingly overwhelming odds and challenges.

"So shall My word be that goes forth from My mouth; It shall not return to Me void, But it shall accomplish what I please, And it shall prosper in the thing for which I sent it" (Isaiah 55:11 NKJV). As stated in this Scripture, the promises of God cannot return void. We invite you to take this journey of faith with us and our fellow Canadians as we present *The Kingdom Promise.*

CHAPTER 2

There Is a God, and It Ain't You!

Gary Gregor and Gerry O'Mahoney

"The LORD brings death and makes alive; he brings down to the grave and raises up. The LORD sends poverty and wealth; he humbles and he exalts."

1 Samuel 2:6–7 NIV

One of my favourite people is Gary Gregor, who farms outside Moose Jaw.

Gary is also a psychologist, with a passion for helping people. When he was working in the community college system in his home province of Saskatchewan he was seeking a way to assist young people so they could get better results and succeed.

This led him into exploring how he could use his knowledge of how our brains function in order to stimulate better outcomes, and what he learned he applied to help people with their challenges.

Saskatchewan is Canada's agricultural heartland, and Gary conducts seminars for farm families, many of whom have been decimated by low commodity prices that have created economic hardship and in many instances have caused them to lose farm assets that had been in their families for generations. He provides comfort and hope for these people.

He also acts as a consultant for Fortune 500 companies and as a strategist across North America.

In addition to all of these things, he is a brilliant sports psychologist, who helped the Saskatchewan Roughriders win the 1989 Grey Cup (only their second of three titles in their 100-year history).

He would tell people, "There's two things you need to know: there is a God, and it ain't you!"[1] I always got a big laugh out of this because it captures the plain-spoken but wise attitude of people who live on the Canadian prairies. As farmers they truly understand the key principles of the kingdom of God, which is that all crops and great harvests come from seed and that the seed must be nurtured, watered and tended as the crop grows and flourishes, and eventually there will be a harvest in the fall.

But it is not the farmer who transforms the tiny seeds into endless fields of golden wheat that feeds the world, but the mighty God of Israel. The farmer understands he must live on faith, the belief that God will provide, that despite rain, wind, drought, hail, frost, insects, weeds and all kinds of strife and hardship, God will deliver the crop and give them the faith at the end of every season to believe to plant again in the spring, sometimes against all worldly reason, including hard-hearted bankers and indifferent government officials and greedy commodity speculators.

> *This is what the kingdom of God is like. A man scatters seed on the ground. Night and day, whether he sleeps or gets up, the seed sprouts and grows, though he does not know how. All by itself the soil produces grain—first the stalk, then the head, then the full kernel in the head. As soon as the grain is ripe, he puts the sickle to it, because the harvest has come.* (Mark 4:26–29 NIV)

The point is that when facing an oncoming storm we need to get our perspective right. If there is no God, then it's every man and woman for themselves. However, if it's true—and we fervently believe it is—that there is a God and it ain't you, then we need to figure out what this means and how we react to it. We also have to remember who created the universe and who is in charge, and it wasn't the result of some "big bang" or arbitrarily concocted evolution theory.

Come on, the house you live in wasn't built by the house; it was built by a builder. The universe wasn't built by the universe; it was designed and built by a creator.

Sir Frederick Hoyle, the late noted British scientist—not a theologian—put it this way: "The probability of life originating on earth is no greater than the chance that a hurricane sweeping through a scrap-yard would have the luck to assemble a Boeing 747."[2]

In fact this concept was echoed by Albert Einstein when he was asked if he believed in God. Now with the rampant growth of atheism in the Western world led by those who favour science over faith like Richard

Dawkins, the Cambridge University professor, scientist and non-believer who wrote the best-selling *God Delusion*, and the late Christopher Hitchens, another Brit who wrote a best seller called *God Is Not Great*, many skeptics would have expected Einstein to reject the concept of God.

However, here is what Einstein, who is recognized to be the smartest man to live in recent times, said to the God question:

> I'm not an atheist…We are in the position of a little child entering a huge library filled with books in many languages. The child knows someone must have written those books. It does not know how. It does not understand the languages in which they are written. The child dimly suspects a mysterious order in the arrangement of the books but doesn't know what it is. That, it seems to me, is the attitude of even the most intelligent human being toward God. We see the universe marvellously arranged and obeying certain laws but only dimly understand these laws.[3]

Even though he was raised as a Jew, Einstein had a great attraction to Christ: "As a child I received instruction both in the Bible and in the Talmud. I am a Jew but I am enthralled by the luminous figure of the Nazarene."[4]

He went on to say he accepted the historical existence of Jesus: "Unquestionably! No one can read the Gospels without feeling the actual presence of Jesus. His personality pulsates in every word. No myth is filled with such life."[5]

We need as humans to deal with this situation and make sure we line up properly with our Creator so we can fulfill our purpose here on earth and have a happy and productive life.

The key point is that God is sovereign and so we must defer to him, as he will not defer or adjust to us. *"For I am the LORD, I change not"* (Malachi 3:6 KJV). This is difficult for us as humans with our egos to deal with and accept.

Gerry O'Mahoney is both a successful business and spiritual leader. He was the SVP of TD Bank Financial Group in Canada and chief operating officer of TD Waterhouse, one of Canada's top brokerage houses, with 1,800 employees under his leadership.

On the spiritual front, Gerry for the last 25 years has been a key speaker in the Leadership Impact Group (founded by Paul Henderson and part of the Power to Change ministry). Gerry is also a well respected member on the board of World Vision Canada.

Gerry, despite his "worldly" success, is a committed Christian who understands the concept of deferring to and obeying God.

"I think surrender, really, is the real action that comes out of accepting the fact that I am not God, that God is God. And I think that we're required to surrender to demonstrate our ongoing commitment to follow him.

"I developed the daily practice of continuously turning my mind to God. In the morning, at noon and throughout the day at work I take a moment and acknowledge God. I ask God to be present in me and to provide his guidance for me. God's support and direction has made it much easier for me to make important business decisions and lead with confidence as a VP.

"I have learned to surrender my life, with all its professional and personal challenges, to God. Resting in God's love and strength has given me the confidence to strive to be my best every day.

"The challenge is, and like our human nature, we are exhorted today to be self-made successful people. Frankly, that's probably not the best place to be.

"I heard a great line one time. Someone said, 'Well you know, he's a self-made man and he worships what he has created.'

"And I think the danger with how we're approaching life today is we're continually looking for those trappings of success around us. And I think we're all prone to that. I know I am, and I want what's best for me, I want what's best for my family, I want what's best for them in their careers as they start to work, et cetera, et cetera. So it's a continuous desire for us to be successful and to want to show that somehow.

"I don't think that's where God is. When you read about the lives of the saints, you certainly don't see that at all. They were not trying to be as great as possible before men; they were trying to be as humble as possible before God, and he turned them into great people.

"It's hard to keep our trust in God because we don't see him physically; we don't hear his voice—at least I don't. Some people do, some people are given the gift of locution, some people are given visions, but that hadn't been my experience in life. So we see by faith, not by sight. And that's hard.

"I'm always amused at people thinking that the Christian walk is easy. I think the Christian walk is incredibly hard, and harder the longer you walk in it and the more you expose yourself to what God says. Especially with the guidance of a good spiritual coach, I think that we get to see more of where God is working around us.

"So that daily trusting, I think, is something that we've just got to get more and more tuned in to; it only happens by listening in and tuning in. But God is going to be incredibly faithful if—like the Scripture says in Revelation, he knocks on the door, and if we open it, he'll come in."

Gerry O'Mahoncy and Gary Gregor, one an immigrant from Ireland, the other a farmer from Moose Jaw, have both learned the key truth in life, that no matter who you are, God is the boss.

[1] Gary Gregor acknowledges the idea for this quote came from the 1993 movie "Rudy" from Tri-Star Pictures.

[2] Frederick Hoyle, *The Intelligent Universe* (London: Michael Joseph, 1983), 18–19.

[3] Max Jammer, *Einstein and Religion* (Princeton, Princeton University Press, 2002), 48.

[4] Ibid., 22.

[5] Ibid.

Chapter 3

Seek Ye First the Kingdom

David Mainse

"Seek ye first the kingdom."

Matthew 6:33 KJV

Human beings are needy.

We all need basic resources, both physiologically and psychologically, to survive and thrive in this world. It is the meeting of these needs and our ability to conquer them that define us. It also is what motivates us.

This book is about the Kingdom Promise and as such includes great truths revealed in the Bible through Jesus and other biblical figures, like King Solomon, and how we can apply these principles today to transform our lives.

However, before we delve into this, let's look at how the world sees need and how we as human beings tend to deal with this issue.

This was best chronicled by an American psychologist named Abraham Maslow, who in the 1940s created a formula in the shape of a pyramid called Maslow's hierarchy of needs.

Maslow's Hierarchy of Needs

The essence of Maslow's contention is that human beings must by necessity prioritize their needs.

At the base of the pyramid are our fundamental physical needs (air, water, food, sleep and excretion). The contention is that until we have these basic needs conquered (and let's be honest, we know that a large percentage of the world's population don't), we can't progress to the next level.

The second level is safety, which is both physical, the lack of real threats like war and natural disasters, and psychological, the peace of mind of knowing that you and your family have a degree of financial and emotional security.

The third level is love/belonging. This again has physical and psychological aspects in that we have a physical need for mating, procreation, which is balanced with an emotional need for love, intimacy and family.

The fourth level is esteem, which relates to our self-image, how we see ourselves in the world. This includes our sense of accomplishment, confidence and ability to move in the world (our career, social position, etc.).

The fifth and final level was defined by Maslow as being self-actualization, which is at the highest rung of human existence from his perspective and deals with values and higher levels of thinking and existence, like morality and creativity.

Maslow went on to hypothesize that human beings move through this pyramid from bottom to top and that basically you can't progress to another level until the level that you are at has been conquered.

Maslow's hierarchy of needs is a perfect characterization of how the "world" sees human needs. But the key to the Kingdom Promise is to see how God sees these things, and it is totally opposite.

What Jesus did, almost 2,000 years before Maslow got around to his version, set this whole notion on its ear. What Christ says to believers takes Maslow's hierarchy of needs and turns it upside down.

He says to forget directly pursuing all of these earthly needs and seek God first in your life! *"But seek ye first the kingdom of God, and his righteousness"* (Matthew 6:33 KJV).

In Maslow's pyramid, "self-actualization," which is a fancy academic way of saying spiritual fulfillment, can only come after all the other four rungs of the structure have been climbed. But as we recently acknowledged, probably a large percentage of the world's current population can't get the basic needs of the first stage: air, water, food and shelter. So in reality this is a true "mug's game" in the sense that it is set up for you to fail. How many "secular" people ever make it to the top of the pyramid?

Jesus even admonished people who indulged in this behaviour with the following: *"(For after all these things do the Gentiles [ungodly] seek:) for your heavenly Father knoweth that ye have need of all these things"* (Matthew 6:32 KJV). His point was simple: all earthly desires and needs will be fulfilled when you surrender and obey your Father who is in heaven.

Therefore, the acquisition of these things comes as a by-product of your righteousness, not as a result of a direct pursuit of these goals.

Furthermore, Jesus instructed us directly not to worry about any of these things, because God will see to it that his "flock" of sheep are provided for.

I feel that it is important to excerpt the whole passage in Matthew 6 and for you to read and meditate on this and even, as my colleague Pastor Neleitha Hewitt says, "Read it aloud, and get it in your spirit."

> *Therefore I say unto you, Take no thought for your life, what ye shall eat, or what ye shall drink; nor yet for your body, what ye shall put on. Is not the life more than meat, and the body than raiment? Behold the fowls of the air: for they sow not, neither do they reap, nor gather into barns; yet your heavenly Father feedeth them. Are ye not much better than they? Which of you by taking thought can add one cubit unto his stature? And why take ye thought for raiment? Consider the lilies of the field, how they grow; they toil not, neither do they spin: And yet I say unto you, That even Solomon in all his glory was not arrayed like one of these. Wherefore, if God so clothe the grass of the field, which to day is, and to morrow is cast into the oven, shall he not much more clothe you, O ye of little faith? Therefore take no thought, saying, What shall we eat? or, What shall we drink? or, Wherewithal shall we be clothed? (For after all these things do the Gentiles seek:) for your heavenly Father knoweth that ye have need of all these things. But seek ye first the kingdom of God, and his righteousness; and all these things shall be added unto you. Take therefore no thought for the morrow: for the morrow shall take thought for the things of itself. Sufficient unto the day is the evil thereof.* (Matthew 6:25–34 KJV)

This passage, I believe, is one of the most powerful in the whole Bible and is the key to the Kingdom Promise.

God is telling us, "Seek me, and I, the God of Israel, through my beloved son Jesus Christ and the Holy Spirit, will fulfill all of your earthly needs."

Furthermore, have faith and stop worrying. The simple fact is that worry is the diametric opposite of faith. If you have stress or worry, it means that you lack faith in God to deliver you.

But how does the Kingdom Promise of Matthew 6:33 manifest itself in our lives in a practical manner? What does "*seek ye first the kingdom*" mean, and how does one go about doing it?

To answer this we want to turn to Dr. David Mainse, the iconic Canadian evangelist who both founded Crossroads Christian Communications, which has been a staple of Canadian television and international Christian media for five decades, and hosted the daily television show *100 Huntley Street.*

It has been so successful that he has built it into an entire broadcast network, CTS, seen across the country, whose operations are housed in the magnificent Crossroads Centre, which he spearheaded and built in Burlington, Ontario.

But aside from all of his accomplishments and accolades, which are too numerous to mention, Dr. Mainse is still the humble small-town pastor from Ontario who started out giving late-night faith-based segments on a tiny television station in Pembroke, Ontario, almost half a century ago.

This is how Dr. Mainse seeks the kingdom of God and his righteousness in his daily routine: "The only way to really meet with God is—well, two ways. With people, other people who pray with you, and to get alone with God. Let God speak through the reading of the Word, and then go into prayer. Let God talk first, read his Word, and go into prayer.

"When I would be in a place of really great need, or the ministry, I'd be kicking up my rising time, and most of the time it was around four a.m. So I could get to our studios, whether downtown Toronto or here in Burlington at the new Crossroads Centre—well, it's not new anymore. At my age, it seems new, but it was 20 years ago now. I would come in early and earlier and earlier, and I would pray.

"Let God speak through the reading of the Word, and then go into prayer. Let God talk first, read his Word, and go into prayer.

"In fact, before we started the daily program—we had 90 minutes a day back in '77—I believe I heard the Lord say, 'David, if you don't spend at least an hour and a half with me every morning before you go on the air, it'll be just you going out there instead of you and me together. So I need an equal amount of time in prayer and meditation and the reading of the Scriptures to what you're going to spend on the air. Otherwise, it will just be you doing the talking, and it won't be you and me together, if you don't spend that time in prayer.'"

This is exactly what the Kingdom Promise is, "seeking God first," reading his Word, meditating on it and then following up in prayer to draw upon his divine wisdom, which we need to direct us in all aspects of our lives. This is eternal advice from Jesus but doubly important as we face difficult times.

CHAPTER 4

And All These Things Shall Be Added Unto You

Joel Auge and Bryan Freeman

Most people believe that God is not interested in money, but nothing could be further from the truth. In fact there are 2,350 mentions of money matters in the Good Book, which makes it the number-one topic, ahead of salvation, morality, death and prayer, in the Word of God.

That's why this book is so relevant; if the issue is the economy and tough economic times, the place to go for answers is the Bible.

Jesus himself referred to money in about 15 per cent of his red letter comments (those attributed to him in the synoptic Gospels), and almost half of his parables referred to economic matters, relating to money and possessions.

It is very clear that money and our management of it is seen, and correctly so, as a barometer of how we live our lives. Are we faithful with our money? Do we pay our tithes, taxes and bills? Do we honour our commitments to God and man?

Are we industrious? Jesus' parable of the talents is very clear that we are to go out in the world and use our God-given gifts for creating wealth. *"His master replied, 'Well done, good and faithful servant! You have been faithful with a few things; I will put you in charge of many things. Come and share your master's happiness!'"* (Matthew 25:21 NIV).

So the issue is that we as Christians should not be disinterested in or ignore economic issues but rather should understand the true purpose of money in our lives. We are to manage money for good, not have it manage and control us.

We can't love money and God, for we will love one and hate the other.

However, the reality for most of us is that we have obligations to family, friends and work that we must honour. People are counting on us, and we don't have the luxury of ignoring them.

The good news is that, as we see in the Scripture in Matthew 6, God understands this. He knows we need provision for shelter, food, transportation and resources to build a life for ourselves and our families, and he is committed to seeing that his followers and believers who obey him receive it. The key point is that, going back to Maslow, the priority in our life is to seek him first, and provision will follow.

As an example of this we want to introduce you to Joel Auge and Bryan Freeman, two young entrepreneurs from Toronto, Ontario, who founded the HitGrab organization (www.hitgrab.com), which has become one of the world's most successful in the emerging area of developing social games.

Bryan always had the gift of an entrepreneurial spirit. Even when working for other companies, he knew that God had a plan for him that was greater than his own expectations. His adventurous spirit had brought him to Canada, to a wonderful marriage, but doing something on his own was terrifying. It took a real leap of faith to follow God's urging to try something. As he prayed about it for over a year, he prayed that he wouldn't have to do it alone. Then Joel started working at the same company as Bryan, and Bryan knew this was who he wanted to partner with.

Joel and Bryan began by starting a business, and a year later they created a hit game called Mousehunt. While this was a big step for these two men, they were very aware that they could not do anything great without God's guidance. God provided the right idea at the right time and the right resources.

Starting a business was a challenging experience for both men, as they had families to support and other commitments. They began meeting in Joel's living room in his little house in Oakville as they threw ideas back and forth. Meanwhile their wives were supporting them financially, spiritually and emotionally.

The first step was to generate some income, but it wasn't enough to support them long term. The second step was to take a loan from the bank and to hire two employees. This added risk meant that they would need to be able to pay their employees' wages when the business wasn't even financing their own incomes.

Another challenge was changing the focus of the business. Originally, they were doing client-orientated work for individuals, but this was not going to pay off long term. They were over-leveraged, using their full lines of credit on credit cards and the bank loan. Unfortunately, they were going to need to let someone go, which would be a devastating setback.

What followed was a serious time of prayer. On his way to a Super Bowl party, Bryan felt moved to pray seriously for God's help. A few nights later, he woke up in the middle of the night with a picture of the HitGrab game in his head. The vision gave him a strong impression of a basic game idea that would work, and it has. It was a real gift from God.

Bryan Freeman explains, "We started experimenting on Facebook, and I was in my car and I said, 'Lord, you know, I really want this to work and I don't want to let that guy go, but we really need your help, right now, you know. And we need some intervention of some sort.' And a few days later I woke up in the middle of the night (which doesn't happen to me), and I had a picture of this game, and I took it to the guy the next day. I was told I was nuts, but we did it anyway, and that game has brought us much success so far.

"So it wasn't a vision, and it wasn't like writing on the wall or a stamp in my mind with great detail or anything. But it was a very, very strong impression of a basic game idea that would work. I just had a very basic concept of how this could work, and everything fell into place. And it's been a real gift from God. This game idea from God and Joel's incredibly good looks have brought us this far, you know."

These two young men, really just starting out in life, put it all on the line to trust God that they could build something on their own and be successful, and because they sought God first, they have built an incredible business that has given them worldwide accolades in a growing field.

So what lessons have they learned? Joel elaborates, "It's been a consistent showing of God's grace in my life that keeps me aware of it, and I really would screw up badly if I was just trying to do it on my own. If we think about God's community of believers, God makes it pretty clear that you need the hand and you need the eye and you need the ear—the full body is required to really live fully. And so I just had this deep-seated knowledge that if I'm going to be effective, then I'm going to have to do it with people who are talented and committed to being there along the way and help me deliver at least my portion. Certainly, it's impossible to do it alone, I think."

If you are entering an era of even greater financial crisis, you need to build up your faith to strengthen yourself for the storm. Whether you are a young entrepreneur like Bryan or Joel or a senior worried that you won't have enough provision to meet your basic needs, the Kingdom Promise remains the same: seek God first, and the things you need will come to you as a by-product of that commitment!

CHAPTER 5

The Kingdom Culture

Mel Stevens

"And do not be conformed to this world, but be transformed by the renewing of your mind, that you may prove what is that good and acceptable and perfect will of God."

Romans 12:2 NKJV

As Christians, we are meant to be distinct and unique from others. We proclaim "kingdom citizenship," a covenant that combines the privileges of God's protection and blessings when we are obedient to his commandments and are faithful as a condition of our citizenship. And as such we have our own "kingdom culture" that is distinct from non-Christians.

So what is kingdom culture? What are our common beliefs? What is it that distinguishes Christians from others, and what do we need to do to strengthen this cultural bond for ourselves and our relationship with the rest of the world?

First, Christians are distinctive in both their thinking and their behaviour, because they are compelled to follow the teachings of Christ, which stand in direct contrast to the ways of the world.

Some of these cultural traditions include the principle of forgiving others for their transgressions, being actively involved in charity and helping the poor and needy, and generally pursuing a moral, transparent life based on the principles of personal integrity.

Christians are supposed to be different, to be *"in the world...not of the world"* (John 17:11–14 NKJV). Thus as a believer in 21st century

Canada many times you will find yourself as *"a stranger in a strange land"* (Exodus 2:22 KJV).

Although you are Christian you probably work with, are friends with and have family members who are not, and frequently this can put you at odds with them over any number of issues, from personal morality and ethics to personal behaviours.

This often leads to conflict and can make you subject to ridicule. You can quickly become ostracized, which makes you feel alienated and persecuted (like Christians since the days of Jesus himself). *"Blessed are those who are persecuted for righteousness' sake, For theirs is the kingdom of heaven"* (Matthew 5:10 NKJV).

You must remember that your faith, your "Kingdom Promise," is your secret weapon that will allow you to triumph when all appears lost. It is, as Paul says, your defense against the attacks that inevitably come your way: *"Put on the whole armor of God, that you may be able to stand against the wiles of the devil"* (Ephesians 6:11 NKJV).

So in this context we want to introduce you to Mel Stevens, a devoted Christian and the founder and driving force for 45 years of Teen Ranch Canada, which is a Christian camp for leadership and sports development. It started in Australia and has spread throughout the world, and Stevens has been directly involved in running the Canadian camp in Caledon in southern Ontario and helping establish another in Indonesia.

Mel has also been very involved in sports, having served for years as the chaplain for the Toronto Argonauts. In fact Bruce Smith, whose testimony appears in this book, credits the Bible that Mel gave him when he played for the team with being instrumental in bringing him to Christ after his career with the Argos was over (he points out that initially the only reason he kept the Bible was because his name was embossed on it). Paul Henderson also credits Mel as being pivotal in bringing him to Christ, through their relationship that was formed when Paul got involved with a hockey camp at Teen Ranch.

However, like all success stories, Mel's has humble beginnings. As a young man he was a member of a popular gospel music group called The King's Men, who were associated with the People's Church and on radio across Ontario. When one day it came up in conversation that a mutual Australian friend had returned to Australia to start a Christian camp without success, the entire group decided they should travel halfway around the world to join him. Now this was no small undertaking, as they all sold everything they owned to buy their tickets, and with wives and children in tow, off they went.

Things were going well with the camp project, but since Mel was the only person there with real camping experience, with a sense of God's calling he felt he should be the first full-time resident director of the facility.

However, under the ranch's by-laws the director could not get paid for his services. This was a big problem for a young Canadian living in Australia with a wife and three kids. Logic would have led Stevens to conclude it couldn't work, but he was called by the Kingdom Promise of Matthew 6:33: "*Seek ye first the kingdom of God, and his righteousness; and all these things [material needs] shall be added unto you*" (KJV). So despite the obstacles Stevens was determined to move forward anyway even over the advice of his boss, who was concerned that he wasn't being realistic (he wasn't).

"And I said, 'Mr. Inglis, I appreciate your concern, but we Christians are called to walk by faith. In fact, Hebrews says without faith, it's impossible to please God. And so Janet and I are willing to trust the Lord for our daily needs. I appreciate your concern about being practical, but I don't believe faith is necessarily practical. If it was practical, it wouldn't be faith. So we're willing to trust the Lord.' And he said, 'Well, I'm concerned for you, but God bless you.' So I stepped out of his office door that day, and that's the first time I really knew that I was under God's direction. I just had a peace in my heart and a lilt to my step and said, 'Thank you, Lord.'

"And so that began a walk of faith in Australia for five and a half years where we received no salary, no wages; we never sent out a request for funds, never sent out a prayer letter. But we had a very small amount of donations, and the Lord multiplied them enough, so we raised our family of three kids at that time and for the next five and a half years with just trusting the Lord for our daily needs. And that was wonderful because when we felt that God was leading us back to Canada to start Teen Ranch Canada, we had already experienced five and a half years walking by faith, so it was nothing new to walk by faith when we came back here to start all over again."

Mel then was tremendously successful with Teen Ranch, but there were setbacks. First, Mel's wife, Janet, got cancer and died at just age 49. Then there was another challenge when there was a construction accident at an arena they were building to augment the facility, and the ramifications threatened Teen Ranch's very existence.

A decision had been made that Teen Ranch needed its own arena to enhance the ranch's facilities to attract young hockey players. However, after the construction started and all the beams were up, the structure suddenly collapsed, causing about half a million dollars of damage.

This became a real disaster when after two years they couldn't get any money from the insurance companies and the ranch was not in a position to shoulder these types of heavy losses.

His lawyer, a powerful King Street barrister, told him the only solution to his problems was to sue everybody in sight; however, this was an issue for Mel. That very day in his daily devotions he had been reading 1 Corinthians 6, which says we should not sue a fellow Christian and bring them in front of an unrighteous justice system. He felt the reading was prophetic, because if he followed the lawyer's advice he would have to sue three Christian businessmen as part of the process.

Now in the short term, this didn't work out so well, as without the suits the issue remained unresolved, which meant Teen Ranch would have to shut down. But then something remarkable happened.

"My brother who was a pastor in California called me one day in January and said, 'Mel, I've got a young couple in the church. The guy is a concrete truck driver; his wife is a domestic immigrant from El Salvador. They asked me about that camp in Canada. They didn't know its name was Teen Ranch and they said, "How is that camp going?"' He said, 'For some reason I took the liberty of telling them you're in deep trouble and you could lose the whole ranch ministry.'

"And a couple of days later, they went back to my brother -he didn't really know them that well; it was a big church of 1,500 people, and they came back and said—'We made an investment in some sort of international financing a few years ago, and we told the Lord that any returns from that would be used for his work and we wouldn't keep a penny.' And they said, 'How much would it cost to get that lawsuit settled?' And he said, 'I really didn't know, but I told them $600,000 probably would cover it.' The end of the story is that within a month, we had $822,000 sitting in our bank account in Orangeville—I get a little emotional when I tell this story—and the lawsuit was settled.

"So that's a rather wonderful answer to prayer, desperate, desperate prayer. But God knew, and if we just relax and know that God is sovereign, he is in control no matter what happens. Romans 8:28 says all things work together for the good of those who love him, who are called according to his purpose. And our lives would be less stressful if we mere humans could understand that we have an eternal God who loves us and has his glory, number one, and our good as his interest."

Mel Stevens, 76 years young, is a great testament to the difference one individual can make in the lives of others. When he was advised that he needed to sue the three Christian men involved with the arena project, he declined because of what Paul said in 1 Corinthians: *"Dare any of you, having a matter against another, go to law before the unrighteous?"* (6:1 NKJV)—that suing the brethren was wrong and against God's teachings.

Now that's the kingdom culture. I'm sure the big-time King Street lawyer thought he was nuts, but Mel didn't care; he trusted the Scriptures just as he had in Australia years before when as a young "King's man" he volunteered to head up Teen Ranch with no idea of how he would support his family.

He has accomplished much but dismisses it with the humility that is appropriate for a Christian who sees himself as a simple servant. "Number one, I don't consider myself having great faith or deep devotion. I'm a fellow traveller along the way, often trial and error, but the one key, I think, to some of my relationship with the Lord is availability. I don't consider myself highly intelligent, I've never been wealthy, I've never had brilliant managerial skills. And even as a musician, I would consider myself mediocre. But I've made myself available to the Lord, and consequently I think that's the key to what my relationship with him has been—just being available to be used and trying not to get in his way as we walked the walk of faith."

CHAPTER 6

The Kingdom of Canada

John Arnott

"If My people who are called by My name will humble themselves, and pray and seek My face, and turn from their wicked ways, then I will hear from heaven, and will forgive their sin and heal their land."

2 Chronicles 7:14 NKJV

When we use the term *kingdom of Canada* it has a double meaning. First off, as a member of the British Commonwealth we are a monarchy that recognizes Elizabeth II as our official head of state, but in addition, Canada was established as nation under God's authority and as a place to build God's kingdom here on earth. As an example of this we should examine the evolution of our national anthem, "O Canada."

Most of us are familiar with the line "God, keep our land glorious and free," but you may not know that there are additional verses to the song. Consider these lyrics and you will see that in its early days it was very clear whose jurisdiction the young dominion was under:

Ruler supreme, who hearest humble prayer,
Hold our Dominion in thy loving care;
Help us to find, O God, in thee
A lasting, rich reward,
As waiting for the better day,
We ever stand on guard.[1]

This should come as no surprise. The Christian faith was fundamental to Canada's development, starting with French missionaries who helped settle

Quebec and then English missionaries who moved north after the American Revolution and introduced Protestantism to what was then a British colony.

Christian fervour probably peaked in the 1950s when almost 70 per cent of Canadians attended church, which at the time was higher than even in the United States.

However that was then, and today Statistics Canada estimates that weekly attendance is just over 20 per cent and, more alarmingly, that seniors make up a disproportionate segment. To gain insight into this we turn to John Arnott, one of Canada's foremost pastors, teachers and spiritual leaders, of world renown. John and his lovely wife, Carol, are the founding pastors and presidents of Catch the Fire in Toronto, formerly known as Toronto Airport Christian Fellowship. It's a citywide church with over 10 locations and about 2,000 vibrant members.

The Airport Church is where the "Toronto Blessing," which the Arnotts oversaw, occurred during the 1990s, which created a charismatic revival that reverberated around the globe.

They're also presidents of Catch the Fire World, which is their international church planting and outreach arm for conferences, schools and soaking prayer centres in churches. Also, they're the overseers of Partners in Harvest and Friends in Harvest, their church network of over 500 churches in over 40 nations.

John is an international speaker and is known for his ministry of revival in the context of a father's saving and restoring love as well as the Holy Spirit moving with signs and wonders, which has seen millions of people's lives touched and changed through God's power and Christ's love. In a recent interview with Gary, John spoke of the changes that are happening in both Canada and the world.

"I think the wheat and the weeds are coming into maturity. The wheat is getting more and more mature, and so are the healthy plants. In other words, the kingdom of God is getting to be like it's never been since 2,000 years ago, and yet the weeds and the problems are also reaching maturity, and we've got greater problems than we have ever had.

"There are a lot of things that are shaking right now, like the morality of the nation, the finances of the nation, the economy of the nation, the threat of diseases and problems. I mean, we're out of fish, we're out of clean water, we're out of this and that and the other. There's just a lot of problems when you start factoring them all in, and then terrorism and nuclear Iran, and Israel's situation, potential wars, existing wars. I mean, there's a lot of things that could give us some very serious problems. I think it goes back to our own morality. If we would come back to God in terms of a nation-shaking revival, that would put the brakes on all the other stuff, I think, because God is good and he's faithful, and that's his heart, that's what he wants to do.

"But at the same time there's biblical prophecy and fulfillment about the coming of the Lord and the end-time scenario, and we may well be in the last days. We do our best in terms of bringing the kingdom of God to earth and being good stewards of what he's given us and taking our talents and investing them and seeing that multiply, but yet, one day, he will come! He will return!

"The fact that Israel is a nation once again is something that had been prophesied over and over and over, probably a score of times if not more in the Old Testament, that the ancient Jewish people would one day be back in their same land, and there they are now, since '48, in that land. So they're in the same ancient lands, speaking the same ancient language, following the same ancient religion. When has that ever happened to any other nation before? But this is the second time for Israel.

"And then there's another prophecy from Jesus, in Luke 21:24, that the city of Jerusalem would be occupied by the nations of the world until the times of those nations were fulfilled. Jerusalem was captured and taken by Israel in 1967, and I can remember watching that on the news, and that was an amazing thing. I did not have CNN then, but we had news coverage, and so that was it.

"Jesus also said the gospel of the kingdom will be preached in all the nations and then the end will come. The gospel has gone to every nation. There are Christians in every single nation on earth, and it's getting there more and more by television and Internet and electronic media, etc. So there is revival today, even in countries like Iran, of all places. It is phenomenal what's happening in the Middle East, in Africa, in Asia and China and India, Indonesia, certainly the South Korea story, and Latin America. Everywhere is ablaze with the gospel except the Western world, and that's a concern, but it also fulfills that great falling away prophecy. So I think in general terms, we are in the last days, and the wheat and the weeds are growing together."

It is clear that Canada is following Europe's lead in becoming a post-Christian secular society, but at what cost? Is spiritual bankruptcy a precursor to financial bankruptcy?

It is interesting that there is a relationship between the Christian faith and prosperity. When Europe was predominant in the world, it was during an era when Christian churches were strong. The greatest empire in history was the British Empire, which at its height covered almost a quarter of the world's land and a fifth of the world's population. It was said that "the sun never set on the British Empire," which was literally true because it was always daytime somewhere in one of their colonies.

We believe that the British Empire was established to conquer the globe and its resources for imperial purposes and to enrich England. However, while of course that is true, historians note that the real motivation for colonial expansion was Christian evangelism and carrying out the great commission to take the gospel to all corners of the earth.

It is worth noting that with the dramatic rise of secularism in post-World War II England, its strength and influence has diminished to an all-time low. Cause or effect?

Christianity is now growing at a much higher rate in the Third World, in Africa, South America and Asia. In fact, now the Third World is sending missionaries to Europe to evangelize the lost.

The question facing Christians in Canada is what role they will play in building revival. As reflected in the Bible verse at the start of this chapter, 2 Chronicles 7:14, there is a collective responsibility in terms of faithfulness and righteousness. In the Old Testament the children of Israel were constantly falling out of favour with God because of their rebellion and disobedience. This had an impact on all the people of Israel regardless of their individual righteousness. *"He causes his sun to rise on the evil and the good, and sends rain on the righteous and the unrighteous"* (Matthew 5:45 NIV). In simple terms, we're all in this together, and if the secular forces in our nation want to drive Canada over the cliff, we're all destined to go along for the ride.

So then as we go through the transition, we need to consider our corporate responsibility, not only to ourselves, our families and our friends but also to our country, to be good citizens and fight for the values and beliefs that define us. *"Be watchful, and strengthen the things which remain, that are ready to die"* (Revelation 3:2 NKJV).

[1] "O Canada," music by Calixa Lavallée, English lyrics by Robert Stanley Weir.

CHAPTER 7

Chazown

David Mainse's Perfect Vision

"Where there is no vision, the people perish: but he that keepeth the law, happy is he."

Proverbs 29:18 KJV

"For I know the plans I have for you," declares the LORD, "plans to prosper you and not to harm you, plans to give you hope and a future."

Jeremiah 29:11 NIV

The purpose of the *Trusting Through the Transition* series is to prepare people for the challenges and potential problems that lie ahead. In this initial publication, *The Kingdom Promise,* we begin by outlining a spiritual foundation to strengthen and fortify our faith so we can be ready and confident to meet the future head on.

The good news is found in verses like the one just quoted from Jeremiah. God has plans for us, and they are good plans to help us today and in the future.

However, the logical question that arises out of this is "How do we connect with God's plan for our lives?" It is clear that God's plan is best, but if we are deceived and take the wrong path or direction, the results are unlikely to be good. And if we are heading for tough times, obviously we don't want to head down a dead-end at a time of crisis.

So how do we tap into the Lord's plan? The answer is found in an old Hebrew word, *chazown,* which means "vision" or "revelation."

The fact is that you are unique and unlike any other human being on the planet. That's why you're here—because God has a purpose for your life that no other person can accomplish. Furthermore, you have a talent or gift to accomplish this purpose that no other human being has or has in the same quantity.

However, here's the problem: most of us don't know what our purpose is or what our gifting is, and as a result we go through life unfulfilled and unhappy. And probably more often than not we delude ourselves; we want things for ourselves based on what we see getting the greatest accolades from a worldly perspective.

The answer to "What is the divine purpose of our lives?" will always have a common factor: God's purpose for our lives will always involve us helping build his kingdom on earth. Now here's the interesting part: God reveals these purposes and callings through visions, or *chazown,* so we are able to know not only our purpose but also how we are able to accomplish it and what his planned outcome is.

The problem is that today most of us want to use our "free will" to create a self-made vision that fits our own perception of who and what we should be. Then many of us who are Christians go to God to get him to "affirm" our plan and then are devastated when it doesn't happen. We even get mad and blame God for its failure.

We are doing things backwards; we need to go to God for the plan, because he knows the true purpose for our lives. Furthermore, when we get in alignment with God's plan we will have the best outcome.

To this point we want to cite the testimony of Dr. David Mainse, who is arguably Canada's best known evangelical leader, the founder and on-air host from 1977 to 2003 of *100 Huntley Street,* the daily one-hour Christian program seen nationally on Global Television.

The program *100 Huntley Street* is produced through his company Crossroads Christian Communications, which also evolved into its own national television network, CTS, headquartered in Burlington, Ontario.

Obviously, David Mainse had a *chazown* to build this broadcasting network in Canada, but what was the process, and what gave him the faith to follow this very daunting and ambitious vision?

The answers are apparent in an interview Mainse recently gave to Gary Gradley. David was born into a religious family with a theologian father; however, his early years did not indicate that he was on the straight and narrow.

"My dad was a professor of theology, Dr. Roy Mainse. Our mealtimes were kind of question-and-answer in theological and current events, and we prayed on our knees three times a day. But then my mother died when I was 12, and I turned out to be a bitter teenager. By the time I was 15, I was kicked out of the religious boarding school where I had been placed.

"I got into a regular high school, and at 16 I made my lifetime decision as a result of other boys in my high school class who were strong in their faith, true blue, excellent character, and I thought I wanted to be like those guys. I was going the other way, so it resulted in me going forward at The Ottawa Auditorium at a Youth for Christ rally to commit my life to Jesus Christ, and I've never looked back.

"Then that summer I turned 17. Well, I really had an experience with the Holy Spirit, not unlike that which launched the Church on the day of Pentecost, and I knew God had called me into the ministry. In fact, I would tell God in prayer, 'God, I would love to be able to serve you full time, as my full-time job,' and the Lord responded by giving such a clear call to the ministry that I could never have done anything else."

The circumstances here are not that unique among second generation pastors, but what was it that drew him to be a clarion for Christian broadcasting? There was no media involvement in his background, and in the early 1950s he knew virtually nothing about the emerging technology of television.

"Well, I certainly didn't know it was going to be television. In fact at that time I'd never seen television in my whole life. No, I take it back. I had a sister who lived in Buffalo, New York. They had a little old grainy, snowy black-and-white TV when I went to visit her when I was 15.

"But, no, that would have never crossed my mind, and I became a school teacher, a public school teacher in Ontario. I was just 18, but by that time I had enough education that I qualified...I wanted to earn some money before I went on to study in Bible college, but that was a great training ground in that classroom in Chalk River, Ontario.

"We went on from there and bit by bit came back into that area again. Pembroke, Ontario, is where we began the television ministry. Then our first programs, our first Saturday night, 11:30 p.m., the original *Saturday Night Live* if you will because they had no taping facilities. They had one camera. You did it live in that new TV station or you didn't do it at all. And 11:30 p.m., first Saturday night of June 1962.

"Everybody was getting a black-and-white TV, and they could pick it up. Aerials were appearing out of the roofs all the way along the Trans-Canada

Highway, and so I saw that as a great opportunity. Actually, I had been visiting door-to-door throughout Deep River, which is the residential area for Atomic Energy of Canada. Sometimes I was welcomed. Sometimes I wasn't welcomed. But I thought, now here's a non-threatening way to visit people, and if they want, they can turn their TVs off.

"Of course we were sneaky, between the late news and sports, which came up from Toronto, and the only late movie of the week, which was played off of film by the Pembroke station. If they were going to watch the only late movie of the week, they had to watch our Crossroads telecast first. And when I would drive home, all the lights were on. You know, they were all watching the only late movie of the week, 26 miles up the highway to Deep River. And so that's how it went, and it was with a goal of helping people.

"In fact there was a man in Deep River who was an alcoholic, and he promised me he was going to watch. Well, shortly after, maybe the second or third Saturday night, I got a phone call at 4:30 in the morning. And I had visited him in his home—alcoholic, family left him. It was just too tough for them. And he promised me he would watch faithfully every Saturday night. Now, he was probably three sheets to the wind, but he was going to watch. He'd keep his word, I knew. He was a good man.

"It was about 4:30 in the morning when my phone rang, and 'Hello, David? This is Ed.' 'Ed,' I said, 'are you drunk?' 'No,' he said, 'I'm not. I tried that and it didn't work.' He said, 'I just got off my knees. I've been on my knees for about an hour talking to God, and I believe that God has come into my life. That he's changed my life, and I'm going be a new man from here on in.'

"Well, I got over to church that Sunday, stood up and told the congregation what he had done during the night, and...we've never changed. Actually, the format has been the same ever since. It's the same format roughly with a lot more variety now, of course, on the daily *100 Huntley Street* telecast—daily and nightly, nine o'clock every night, on CTS, of course."

Today it's hard to imagine that the man behind a major broadcasting empire emanating out of Burlington, in a state-of-the-art 143,000 square foot facility he built and was able to get financed, came from the humble beginnings of a late-night broadcast on a small eastern Ontario independent television station, but that's how it happened.

This is a vital point we cannot overlook. When we are working in God's purpose he will bring us the resources we need to accomplish his purpose.

David Mainse puts it best: "Faith, again as I said, is just obedience. That's all you need, enough faith to obey. Don't try to work it out. That's the enemy. If you try to conjure up some more faith or whatever, that's the enemy of real faith. Real faith—find out what the Word of God says, then obey it. Find out what the still small voice says inside; go for it and believe God to throw a monkey wrench in the works if you're not in his plan.

"In the whole area of finance, as you pray, God will raise up people. Like the first gift to first go on television back in '62 was the Chrysler dealer in Pembroke, a man by the name of Sid Healey. He called me in. He knew I had a desire to do television on the new TV station. He called me in and gave me a cheque for three hundred dollars. Well, that would be well over two thousand dollars today. And that was the beginning, and Sid was a great man.

"He had a lot to do with my decision. I worked for him part-time back when I was in grade 12 in high school—the time I made my lifetime decision to follow Christ as a result of Sid, as well as those young men in my high school class. So all along the way, the Lord has kind of stepped up to the plate."

Amen, David. Amen.

CHAPTER 8

Don Cherry's Leap of Faith

Every major success story has an element of happenstance that couldn't have been predicted that changes the outcome in a favourable way. However, many times God asks us to do something difficult or unusual to receive our blessing and to believe in the unbelievable, although logic would tell us otherwise.

He told Moses to go back to Egypt, where he was wanted for murder and a refugee from justice, to go to the pharaoh and request that he release the children of Israel. At first Moses resisted, feeling both afraid and unable to do the task.

The concept terrified Moses, who had no idea how he could convince the pharaoh to do this. But God equipped him by giving him miraculous signs so that the Egyptians would know that Moses was blessed with divine powers.

However, most importantly, God was with him, and when God sets about to do something it shall be done, and he will work through people to accomplish his goals.

God told Abraham that he would be the father of many nations even though he was almost 100 years old and his wife, Sarah, was 90. The Bible alludes to the fact that Abraham initially thought God was joking with him about a 100-year-old father and a 90-year-old mother.

But although God definitely has a sense of humour, he wasn't playing here, and Sarah bore Abraham a son, Isaac, the basis of his covenant with the Jewish people (the blessing of Abraham, Isaac and Jacob), which through Christ we as Christians are grafted into.

The key is that faith overcomes all things. But this is tough, because we must learn to live by faith and not by sight. In other words, no matter how bad it looks, how hopeless it seems, God is in the picture, and he will come through for us.

One of the most powerful testimonies I've ever heard is from Don Cherry. Don Cherry is one of the great Canadian icons, a former NHL coach who is now an outspoken commentator on Hockey Night In Canada on Canadian television.

Cherry is so high profile and revered in Canada, he was almost voted the most influential Canadian in history several years ago. Everybody knows Don Cherry, but what is not so well known is Cherry's faith and how it changed his life.

Don Cherry was a career minor league hockey player back in the 1950s, '60s and early '70s and only played one solitary game in the sport's big league, the NHL. Back then, minor league hockey players got paid peanuts and had to work in the off season to support themselves and their families. In Cherry's case he was a construction worker in Rochester, New York, in the off season. Eventually in the late '60s he decided to retire from crisscrossing North America in search of hockey's holy grail and build a life doing construction full time.

However, as he described on the Canadian Broadcasting Corporation's Life and Times,[1] God had another plan for him, something he never could have dreamed of or imagined. In many ways Cherry's journey mirrored Joseph's from the Old Testament, because the first thing that happened after he retired and was now solely relying on his construction job to support him, his wife and children was that he got laid off from that job.

However, he seemed to have overcome this setback when he then landed a job as a Cadillac salesman. For those who know Cherry, he would seem on paper to be the ultimate Cadillac salesman, with his brash demeanour, his outrageous sense of fashion (loud plaid jackets, coloured shirts and bright ties) and his background in Rochester as a popular former hockey star. But this was not his destiny either, and he couldn't for the life of him sell a car. Car salesmen earn a paycheque based on commission from cars sold, but Cherry said on the show that he was "the worst car salesman in the history of the auto industry." Naturally, he became despondent and more than a little anxious, as he was also a very devoted family man, husband and father and wanted to be a good provider.

Finally, at his wits' end, Cherry decided to pray and ask for God's help. He got down on his knees and asked God, "'Is this the end?' I'm 36 years old and I have no future at all and then and believe me I can't stress this too strongly a light came on and I heard a voice say 'you're making a comeback in hockey.'" So following God's direction Cherry went to the office of his old team, the Rochester Americans of the American Hockey League, and begged to get his old job back playing hockey.

Normally, the general manager of the team was never in the office, and this was in the summer, the off season for hockey. But lo and behold, this day he was in.

Remember that Cherry had retired from hockey basically because in his mid-thirties he was considered too old, over the hill. He had been retired for a year. However, Cherry found favour with his old boss. Not only did he take him back, he gave him the biggest contract of his career.

So all summer long Cherry laboured long and hard to get back in shape to play again. His late wife, Rose, described an overweight Cherry huffing and puffing and sweating like a pig in the attic of their home in stifling heat, riding an old exercise bike to get into condition for the upcoming season.

She even said to him, "Don if you keep this up, you're going to die." And he replied, "That's right I'm going to die or I'm going to make this hockey club!"

But when the season started God threw him another curve ball: the team decided partway through the season to fire the coach and replace him.

Minor league sports teams, as I know from personal experience, are notoriously cheap, with money usually in short supply. They decided that rather than hire a full-time coach, they would give the job on an interim basis to Cherry, as they were paying him anyway as a player.

Now this was Cherry's calling. His outgoing personality, penchant for outrageous quotes and fierce competitive nature came to the fore, and he was a hit. The fans loved him. However, once again, as in Joseph's case, there was another setback.

At the end of the season the team in their infinite wisdom decided they wouldn't give the full-time coaching job to Cherry but would hire someone else. However, they were in for a rude awakening. Cherry had found favour with the fans and media; they pitched a fit and bombarded the Americans with complaints until they "repented" and changed their mind and rehired Cherry.

Now Cherry's coaching career was in full bloom. He went on to become a huge success with Rochester, even becoming the American Hockey League "Coach of the Year" and soon the "bigs" came calling. In 1974 Cherry became the coach of the NHL's Boston Bruins.

The Bruins were the kings of the sport of that era. They had won two Stanley Cups and had Bobby Orr, who many consider to be the greatest player to ever lace up skates, plus superstars like Phil Esposito and Gerry Cheevers. Cherry was on top of the world and in 1975–76 was named coach of the year in the NHL.

Remember, this was the same Don Cherry who just a few short years earlier was a washed-up minor leaguer, a fired construction worker and a failed car salesman. So this was a complete turn-around in his life. However, there are key lessons in this story, and it's important to consider each of them.

First, Don recounted to me that when he lost his job in construction he thought it was the "the end of the world" however he now realizes that it was God's plan to get him back into hockey, in that if he hadn't have been fired he never would have considered returning to the sport.

Second, when he heard from God he took a "leap of faith" and did exactly what God had told him.

Cherry succeeded in hockey where he had failed in construction and the car business because hockey was and is his "true passion" where he was called by God to minister.

What Cherry didn't realize was that his gift was not for playing (by his own admission he was not a great player) but for coaching and then even more so later on to be a commentator and ambassador for the sport.

God used the law of attraction in Cherry's life to lead Don Cherry into his destiny. However—and this is vital for all of us to understand—it came with a price and with a lot of adversity.

Don Cherry never would have dreamed that he could have gone back to hockey if he hadn't had an experience through prayer, and secondly he wouldn't have had the conviction to follow through and carry it out. When Cherry started living by faith, everything changed. God gave him favour with the players, the fans and the media; he attracted the attention of the NHL, the league that didn't want him as a player; and he became a super-star coach.

After recounting this story on the Life and Times television show, Cherry looked at the camera, obviously choked up with emotion about how his life was transformed, and said in his signature brusque manner, "And they say there is no God!"

The fact is, Don Cherry knows there is a God and how he can change your life, and what he did for Don Cherry he can do for you.

1 "The Life and Times of Don Cherry," Life and Times, http://www.cbc.ca/lifeandtimes/cherry.html.

CHAPTER 9

In God We Trust

Don Simmonds

"Trust in the LORD with all your heart, And lean not on your own understanding; In all your ways acknowledge Him, And He shall direct your paths."

Proverbs 3:5–6, NKJV

As we apply the Kingdom Promise and seek God first, with the expectation that when we do all of our earthly needs will be met, one of the key factors will be trust.

Frankly, without trust the benefit of the seeking process in Matthew 6:33 will be negated, because complete trust is required to rely on God to keep his promised response.

This is a huge issue, especially in 21st-century Canada where, as we have noted, the kingdom of God is under severe attack.

Thus many Canadians may not activate the Kingdom Promise because they either A) may not believe God exists or B) believe in God, but without the intimate relationship with him that leads to the ability to trust him fully.

That's why we wrote this book, to build Canadian Christians' faith, especially in times of trial, by presenting exceptional testimonials of their fellow countrymen in these pages to get them to the next level.

So what is trust?

I would define *trust* as "I can rely on it, feel confident in it and feel secure in it."

The *Oxford Dictionary* defines *trust* as "firm belief in the reliability, truth, or ability of someone or something."

What do you trust in?

Do you trust in yourself and your abilities?

Do you trust in God—the Creator and Ruler of this world and universe?

Do you trust in others—your fellow human beings?

Do you trust in money—the almighty dollar?

Most people in the developed world, especially in North America, often place our trust in the almighty dollar, our prosperity. We trust that if we have wealth everything will be fine; we feel safe and secure

The national motto of the United States is "In God we trust."

Most of us are familiar with it because it appears, ironically, on their currency.

Jesus spoke about God and money: *"No one can serve two masters. Either you will hate the one and love the other, or you will be devoted to the one and despise the other. You cannot serve both God and money"* (Matthew 6:24 NIV). Do we really trust God completely, or do we place our trust in something or someone else first?

This is a profound and challenging question for most people. We are so programmed by society and our fear-based controlling ego and egoic minds that the thought of giving our control away by trusting totally and relying fully on something else is scary, because we feel out of control and vulnerable.

Our ego will forever resist it, because it will lose control, which is how it operates and survives, through controlling our consciousness. The ego (the flesh) is always fighting against spirit. It has taken me years of working at trusting totally in God. The ego puts up a good fight with all its ways of deceiving us.

I would keep hearing from God,
"Trust me; I will take care of you.
Let go of your fear; let go of your control.
Give it over to me and I will provide perfectly for you.
The more you trust me, the more I will be there to provide."

You may have had at some point a "trust fall" corporate teambuilding experience. In my 22-year career in my corporate training business specializing in experiential learning, I have had the privilege of leading thousands of people through this empowering trust-building experience where you fall backwards from a height into the arms of your team.

Often people are very nervous because they fear getting hurt or failing in front of their peers. When you lean back in a free-fall state you have no control, and the only choice that you really have is to trust that your team with outstretched arms will do their job and catch you safely.

When they do, it builds a tremendous amount of trust within you that you can take a risk and let go, and it builds trust within the team as they demonstrate their care, concern and reliability.

The only good choice and solution is to take the risk and trust. There really is no other option, for if you are going to do it, you must trust!

God is the *only* one worthy of 100 per cent trust, because only God is

omnipotent (all powerful)
omniscient (all knowing)
omnipresent (all present)

Don Simmonds is the chairman and CEO of CTS, a religious television broadcaster, and Crossroads Christian Communications in Burlington, Ontario, which has been a Christian presence in Canadian television for 50 years. Don's business background is as a serial entrepreneur, having been involved in over 20 new ventures in the last 30 years. Don was one of seven partners that started the Lenbrook Group in 1977, a private business incubation company perhaps best known for having created Clearnet, one of Canada's wireless networks, sold in 2001 to Telus.

As well as being a successful business person, Don is a committed family man and Christian, and through an experience with his son he came to understand this process of trusting God more completely.

"It was painful to be away from my children all the time. So on this particular occasion, I decided to take Craig with me on a business trip. He was just four years old, pretty young for such an excursion. But he was a pretty well-behaved four-year-old, so he came with me to Calgary where I had my meetings.

"I used to stay at a hotel there that had these fantastic water slides. And so I planned that if I could finish up my day early, and if he was well behaved, then we would spend the evening on the water slides—which we did. And Craig and I had a whale of a time that day. Over and over we went down the water slides with him sitting in front of me.

"And as we were getting ready to leave I said to Craig, 'Why not try going yourself?' He said, 'No, Dad, no, I'll just go with you.' I said, 'No, I think you're doing so well; why don't you try that yourself?' And so I pushed him hard to go down the water slide by himself, concluding with the statement, 'Trust me. I'll be right here at the bottom when you come down.' And so the little guy went up the steep cement steps where halfway up they turned out of sight. And so I stood at the bottom of the water slide in the foaming water waiting. And I waited. And I waited.

"And I got to thinking, 'I wonder if he's up at the top shivering and some security guard is going, "What are you doing here up alone?" or maybe someone came in from the upper level and took him into their hotel room.' So I said to myself, 'Okay, I'd better just go up and see.' So I got out of that foaming water at the bottom of the waterslide, and I started up the steps to search for him. No one else was using the water slides that evening, but there was a couple sitting on bar stools at the far end of this huge room. Just before I rounded the turn halfway up the stairs, I saw them wave toward me.

"And I took one more look over the railing and saw that Craig had just come down! He was submerged in the foaming water at the bottom of the slide. And so I ran with all my might back down those cement stairs, dived in and pulled him out. Of course, his eyes were as big as saucers. His first words once he got some breath were 'Where were you, Dad?'

"So, here is a loving dad, and I'd asked him to 'trust me,' and, not intentionally by any means, I had let him down completely. In fact, I live with the fact that if I'd gone just a few steps further and hadn't seen those folks wave, the outcome would have been very, very different indeed.

"So here I am, you know, a dad very committed to my children, hoping to have a wonderful time and proved completely fallible. In fact, I proved to Craig to be someone I wouldn't want to recommend he trust 100 per cent. Because I let him down completely!

"It's a story I tell to say that I have learned that God *is* worthy of 100 per cent trust. I can't really say that about any other person or thing that I've encountered in the rest of my life. So you can see that my view of trust in God is big."

Now that's a chilling testimony, a devoted father playing with his four-year-old, that in a moment could have turned tragic. No matter how committed, how careful, how watchful we are, we are flawed, and as our friend Gary Gregor said earlier, "There's a God, and it ain't us!" Ergo we need to put our faith in the divine Creator of the universe.

The question though is, do we have the faith to surrender to him? *"Nevertheless, when the Son of Man comes, will He really find faith on the earth?"* (Luke 18:8 NKJV).

In any crisis, your only real choice is to trust. Trust through the challenge! If you don't, you will perish. For you are not in control. So you ought to trust the one who is in control, and that's God.

> *God is our refuge and strength, A very present help in trouble. Therefore we will not fear, Even though the earth be removed, And though the mountains be carried into the midst of the sea; Though its waters roar and be troubled, Though the mountains shake with its swelling.* (Psalm 46:1–3 NKJV)

Chapter 10

Choosing Faith over Fear

Tim Cestnick

"Therefore I say to you, do not worry about your life, what you will eat or what you will drink...Look at the birds of the air, for they neither sow nor reap nor gather into barns; yet your heavenly Father feeds them. Are you not of more value than they? Which of you by worrying can add one cubit to his stature?"

Matthew 6:25–27 NKJV

We are commanded by Jesus in Matthew 6:33 to seek God first. However, in the preamble to this Scripture he was firm that we are not to worry but to trust his heavenly Father always.

This will come as news to Canadians. As a 2006 Ipsos Reid poll showed, Canada is one of the most stressed-out nations on earth, with over half of Canadians reporting stress in their daily lives that is debilitating and creates major problems.[1]

This emotion of fear is innate in human beings. Its true purpose is for survival, an early warning system designed for our ancestors to warn them of impending danger, be it large predatory animals looking for lunch or invading hordes from a rival tribe looking to perform a little ethnic cleansing.

However, the dangers in the modern world are a little more insidious. What we sometimes categorize as fear is actually anxiety, not because of real, immediate danger but because of a perceived threat that may not even exist.

What are you choosing and experiencing? If you are fear-based, then you are probably feeling worried, concerned, overwhelmed and panicky.

ɔad place to be, a place where you are attracting more bad things ᴊ your life experience. *"For the thing I greatly feared has come upon me, And what I dreaded has happened to me"* (Job 3:25 NKJV). A choice of fear leads you down the road of panic, paranoia, paralysis, depression, hopelessness, pessimism and more loss and suffering.

A choice of faith—full faith and total trust—leads you along the road of hope, optimism, inspiration, positive expectations, belief, action, provision, synchronicity, favour, grace, protection, acceptance, love and peace.

Choosing faith as your foundation is the only way to prevail in a life crisis, including a social-economic crisis.

Faith can be defined as the ability to believe, with strong conviction and complete trust, in something for which there is no initial proof. It is the ability to see the invisible and to believe in the incredible.

David Mainse of *100 Huntley Street* puts it simply: "Faith is just obedience. That's all you need, just enough faith to obey. Find out what the Word of God says and obey it."

The best definition was captured by the apostle Paul: *"Now faith is the substance of things hoped for, the evidence of things not seen"* (Hebrews 11:1 NKJV).

"'Have faith in God,' Jesus answered. 'Truly I tell you, if anyone says to this mountain, "Go, throw yourself into the sea," and does not doubt in their heart but believes that what they say will happen, it will be done for them'" (Mark 11:22–23 NIV). Faith can be powerful; however, there is an enemy that often gets in the way of our faith. The enemy of our faith is our own doubts and fears. Our fears come from our fear-based egoic mind, from past experiences, from our self-talk, from sin and from other's negative talk.

In the book *Experiencing God,* Henry and Richard Blackaby say that everyone in their spiritual journey will experience a crisis of faith. You will come to a point where your faith in God will be tested, and you will need to deliberately decide to totally trust God or distrust God.[2]

It is in this context that we turn to Tim Cestnick, one of Canada's most respected Canadian tax and personal finance experts. He is widely recognized across Canada for his in-depth knowledge, dynamic speaking style, common sense approach and extensive media coverage.

He is also a prolific author. He's written several books, including the Canadian best-sellers *101 Tax Secrets for Canadians, Winning the Tax Game, Winning the Estate Planning Game,* and *The Tax Freedom Zone,* and has co-authored several other books as well. He's also a columnist for the *Globe and Mail's* Report on Business, on tax issues and financial planning.

Cestnick also appears regularly as a radio personality and on TV programs such as *Canada A.M.* and *CBC Newsworld* and on BNN.

"I have the privilege of working with many of the wealthiest families in the country. Many have been concerned in recent days about the stability of their wealth, the impact of the markets on their investments and the economy. The truth is that many Christians share this same concern. My reply to someone who has a personal relationship with God is that, where the Lord is concerned, he is looking after the sparrows, so how much more will he look after us? We can take comfort in this fact. We still have a responsibility to plan properly and make wise decisions with the resources we have, but if we're doing this, then those trusting God can rest assured that their needs will be met financially.

"So regardless of how bad things may get economically or socially in this country or North America, I think we need to have that mindset to say, 'Really, no matter what happens, I'm going to be fine. God will look after me and my family.' This should bring a lot of peace to many people who are otherwise very concerned.

"I strongly believe that if we walk in faith—that is, having a strong faith—and we trust in God, then God will enable and equip us to walk through whatever chaos there is, and to come out the other side stronger. I think I am living proof of that.

"When I left my job at a leading Canadian retail mutual fund company, to create and build WaterStreet Family Offices, I went from having a very high income to having zero income.

"I was never worried about it. God has given me an entrepreneurial spirit, and so taking some calculated risks was something I was comfortable with—particularly because I felt that I was right where God wanted me to be. There's no safer place to be than in the centre of God's will. I always felt confident that God would look after us—and that is exactly what happened.

"There were some huge challenges along the way. During the major economic crisis that the world had to deal with in the fall of 2008 we, as a fledgling business in the financial services industry, faced a significant decline in revenue at a time when we had just made new investments in people and other resources. It really was the 'perfect storm,' and we struggled financially. Our staff were incredible. They understood the challenge we were facing and made sacrifices at that time. As the founder of a business that was struggling, no one was impacted more financially than me.

This put stress on my business partnership and my marriage. There was little I could do in my own strength at that time, and I spent much time in prayer daily.

"I would often pray the 2 Chronicles 20:12 prayer: 'I don't know what to do, but my eyes are upon you.' And God brought about remarkable changes for the better in the business—and my marriage. He really performed a series of miracles in my life at that time. I believe that wholeheartedly, and I think that for people who have a faith in Christ and who are relying on God, he will provide and 'all things work together for good.'

"I need to mention that my wife, Carolyn, has been more understanding than many might have been through the difficult times, and in fact during all of my entrepreneurial ventures. She is a prayer warrior and has always trusted me. I don't think any entrepreneur who is married can survive in business without this type of support."

Tim concludes by saying with conviction, "So if someone finds himself in the midst of a crisis, maintaining that deep faith and total trust is one of the most critical things that he can do in order to position himself for God's provision of improved circumstances."

There is power in facing your fears. As Sir Edmond Hillary, the first man to climb Mount Everest, said, "It is not the mountain we conquer but ourselves." You can avoid much of the fear by building your faith now and firmly trusting in God's perfect plan and provision for you.

As the Ipsos Reid poll shows, the stresses of everyday life are bringing many Canadians to their knees. The question is, are we going to be on our knees praying to God, the divine sovereign of the universe who controls everything, or are we going to be on our knees paralyzed by fear, anxiety and panic, feeling totally helpless and defeated?

The answer should be obvious, but even people who claim to be strong believers can find themselves crippled by fear, and because of this they are unable to accomplish the purpose God has for them and their lives.

"For God has not given us a spirit of fear, but of power and of love and of a sound mind" (2 Timothy 1:7 NKJV). And finally, for a stressed-out nation, the quiet reassurance of the Serenity Prayer: "O God, grant me the serenity to accept the things I cannot change, the courage to change the things I can and the wisdom to know the difference."

[1] "Half of Canadians Say They Have No Control Over Stress Levels," Marketwire, http://www.marketwire.com/press-release/-of-canadians-say-they-have-no-control-over-stress-levels-598798.htm.

[2] Henry Blackaby and Richard Blackaby, *Experiencing God* (Nashville: Life Way Press, 1990).

CHAPTER 11

To Preach the Kingdom of God and to Heal the Sick

Winsome Johnson

"When Jesus had called the Twelve together, he gave them power and authority to drive out all demons and to cure diseases, and he sent them out to proclaim the kingdom of God and to heal the sick."

Luke 9:1–2 NIV

It is clear when we read the Gospels that there was a double mandate. Jesus sent out the disciples armed with the message of the kingdom, plus he gave them the power of healing.

This was consistent with his own ministry; he performed numerous healing miracles, including healing the blind and the deaf, curing leprosy and fever, even restoring a man's withered hand. In one famous passage, in Luke chapter 8, a woman was healed just by touching Jesus' garment, which speaks to the supernatural anointing on him and all that surrounded him.

This culminated with the ultimate healing miracles, raising people from the dead, which he did numerous times, including bringing his friend Lazarus back to life four days after his passing.

Thus, as laid out in the Gospels, Jesus is synonymous with healing. However, the controversial question arises, does Jesus still heal today? If so, where does this fit into the Kingdom Promise?

The answer to this question, as to all questions facing man, is found in the Scriptures. In this case it is found in the writings of the apostle Paul: *"Jesus Christ is the same yesterday, today, and forever"* (Hebrews 13:8 NKJV).

Jesus himself reiterated this point, as is recorded in the last book the Bible, Revelation: *"I am the Alpha and the Omega, the Beginning and the*

End,' says the Lord, 'who is and who was and who is to come, the Almighty'" (1:8 NKJV).

So the point is clear: if Christ is a current and living God, and if he healed in the time of his earthly reign on earth, then he must still heal today, for if he does not, the Scripture would be false, which Christians know is not possible.

Furthermore, Christ's healing powers are a fulfillment of the Scripture of the Old Testament, as he predicted, in which God promised to protect the children of Israel from the disease and afflictions that befell the Egyptians, their captors, who had enslaved them: *"If you diligently heed the voice of the LORD your God and do what is right in His sight, give ear to His commandments and keep all His statutes, I will put none of the diseases on you which I have brought on the Egyptians. For I am the LORD who heals you"* (Exodus 15:26 NKJV).

In this context I want to share with you the testimony of Winsome Johnson and her very personal story of triumph over a life-threatening health crisis. Winsome is a close friend and prayer partner of Pastor Neleitha Hewitt, and what happened to her transformed her life and her faith.

"In 1992, I discovered a lump under my arm one morning while getting dressed for work. I thought nothing of it, but after a few days passed and it was still there I showed it to my husband, who promptly told me, 'Oh, that is nothing to worry about.' A few days later it was still there and I became concerned, so I decided I should visit a doctor a friend had recommended to me. The doctor examined me and told me, 'Don't worry; you don't have breast cancer. You don't show any sign of breast cancer.' He gave me an $80 prescription and an appointment to come back to see him in two weeks. Of course I did not go back.

"Three months later I visited my family doctor because of a pain in my foot. Just before I left his office I said to him, 'By the way, Doctor, please take a look at this lump under my arm.' He examined the area, then sent me for a mammogram. The results came back negative, but he said, 'I don't like to keep lumps on the body, so I will arrange an appointment for you to have day surgery to have the lump removed.'

"The day surgery was a horrible experience. Although freezing was done in the underarm area, I could feel every cut. I screamed, but the surgeon was unsympathetic and spoke matter-of-factly to the anesthetist to freeze it again in a very impersonal tone and just continued with his conversation with the nurses as though I was not there. I was just like an object lying there.

"Two weeks later I went back to the doctor's office to have the bandages removed and to get my clean bill of health to go back to work (or so I thought), only to be told that the tissues that were removed from under my arm were sent for a biopsy and the results were, in his words, 'You have very bad breast cancer of the lymph nodes; also there is a small lump in your breast. Mrs. Johnson, put it this way, you must have major surgery.'

"I immediately wondered who he was speaking to. We were the only ones in the office, but the shock of the moment made me wonder who he was speaking to—not me, of course. I went home like a zombie. At the time my husband was on afternoon shift, and I wanted to tell him before I told anyone else.

"The next day my sister called from work. I preferred not to tell her at work, but as soon as I heard her voice I could not hold it any longer. I just blurted it out. I heard the catch in her voice, then a long silence while I cried. She finally said, 'We will get a second opinion.' That gave me a little hope. Maybe there was some mistake—this doctor was wrong or the lab mixed up the results. Yes, we would get a second opinion.

"In two weeks at Women's College Hospital I had the small lump removed from my right breast and 16 lymph nodes removed from under my arm, and all were cancerous. Again I sat in the doctor's office thinking, 'OK, it's cancer, but I have heard about results like "We got all the cancer out and everything is fine."' But it was not so for me. Instead the doctor said to me, 'Go home and plan your life. There is not much we can do at this point. We will give you chemotherapy and radiation; they may prolong your life, but not for long.' I was diagnosed with stage four aggressive breast cancer.

"That night I decided I must tell my husband. All along he thought it was a cyst. I finally said, 'Honey, the doctor says I have breast cancer.' I saw his knees buckle, and he started to fall. I grabbed him and said, 'Please, do not fall apart on me now. I need you.' I watched him regain strength before my very eyes. He hugged me, saying, 'OK, honey, I will be here.'

"About two years before the diagnosis someone had prophesied to me, saying, 'If you give your heart to the Lord Jesus Christ, he will save the whole family.' Of course I did not believe, and I continued in my sinful lifestyle and refused to commit my life to Jesus.

"After the second surgery and the prognosis from the doctor, I realized I needed help. 'The doctors have done all they can do; now where do I go and what do I do?' I then remembered that a friend had invited me to a church. I had visited a few times, but it was Pentecostal, and I did not like it because of my Baptist background. Now I was desperate. I remembered at that church they would have altar calls for healing or for any desperate need. I visited other churches, but somehow I needed to be at this Pentecostal church.

"My husband and I started visiting the church. One Sunday we were sitting in the service, in a congregation of about 2,000 people. The ministering pastor said, 'There is someone here with cancer who has come for your healing.' Well, I froze in my seat and refused to go up because of pride. I never asked for prayer; I was just too ashamed to tell anyone. Finally I went forward. The pastor prayed for me, then said, 'In the name of Jesus you are healed.'

"Not knowing how to exercise faith, I just dismissed the whole thing. I went for my checkup some time later, and the oncologist at Sunnybrook Cancer Centre told me to go back to see the doctor at Women's College Hospital where I had the surgery.

"I was very concerned, as I thought they were sending me to be set up for more chemo, but to my surprise the doctor said, 'I see they treated you well at Sunnybrook.' I said, 'Yes, they did.' He said, 'Because the cancer is all gone.'

"I felt like this doctor just gave me a million dollars. I had to give Jesus the praise. I said, 'Doctor, this is Jesus; he did this for me,' and the doctor said, 'Of course. We all have to believe in something.' I left the doctor's office rejoicing.

"I shared my good news with my family. It was a happy time for us all. My niece was the first one who gave her heart to our Lord Jesus after my husband. Then our four children, my closest sister and her husband, followed by our three other sisters, then our mother, then close friends gave their hearts to our Lord Jesus Christ, our wonderful saviour. Because of what he did for me we all realized he is real. He is truly a saviour and miraculous healer.

"In 1998 a member of our church was also diagnosed with breast cancer. I called to encourage her because she knew of my healing. One day in our conversation she asked if I attended a support group when I was sick. I told her no, my family was my support. She said, 'I have been to the group at the hospital but was not comfortable. You cannot talk about God, prayers or anything religious.' She asked, 'Would you like to join me in starting a cancer support group?' We prayed about it, and the Lord gave her the name, The Olive Branch of Hope.[1] In April The Olive Branch of Hope, which like AA and other successful organizations is based on kingdom principles, was launched and is now a blessing to many women in our community."

Now this is a very powerful and moving story, with many aspects that are worth examining:

When Winsome was first diagnosed with cancer, she did not believe that the healing power of Christ could save her.

However, as the disease progressed the medical system basically left her without hope and even "prophesied" that she would die very quickly from the stage four cancer.

Something was "attracting" her to a specific Pentecostal church, even though her Baptist upbringing had given her a negative impression of the denomination.

Winsome had to fight with her own pride and suspend her disbelief to "accept" the offer of the pastor to get healed.

Her healing was to a greater purpose. Through this miracle she and her entire family were saved (as was prophesied over her two years before she got sick), and then she and her friend established an organization to help other women with cancer.

This huge obstacle presented Winsome with a life-changing opportunity to come to faith and be a beacon of hope for others and in so doing fulfill the purpose God has chosen for her.

Now we know that at some point all of us will pass away, and many will get sick and pass on. Not everyone gets healed. However, as in the Bible and in the case of Winsome Johnson, miracles are real, and they happen every day. It's important to recognize that faith, like in everything else in the kingdom, is the common denominator.

As the saying goes, "If you don't believe that you can be healed, you're right!"

[1] To find out more about The Olive Branch of Hope go to http://www.theolivebranch.ca.

Chapter 12

Blindsided

Bruxy Cavey

"For yourselves know perfectly that the day of the Lord so cometh as a thief in the night."

1 Thessalonians 5:2 KJV

"And all that believed were together, and had all things common; And sold their possessions and goods, and parted them to all men, as every man had need. And they, continuing daily with one accord in the temple, and breaking bread from house to house, did eat their meat with gladness and singleness of heart, Praising God, and having favour with all the people. And the Lord added to the church daily such as should be saved."

Acts 2:44-47 KJV

As we contemplate an oncoming crisis, there are many challenges; some are physical, some are mental and many are spiritual.

The simple fact is that most of us live in a "comfort zone," which may be a reality but as much as anything is a state of mind.

It is that place where we feel reassured and secure that we are safe; we know who we are and what we're all about and feel a certainty in our existence.

When crises arrive in our life, they threaten our comfort zone and the warm cocoon existence we have built for ourselves, and many times, like the thief in the night who breaks into our home while we are sleeping, they blindside us and catch us unaware and unprepared.

In this regard we turn to Bruxy Cavey. Bruxy is the teaching pastor for The Meeting House. The Meeting House is one of Canada's largest churches, with multiple locations currently across Ontario with thousands of members, and has grown rapidly and dramatically over the last number of years.

He's well-known for his teaching, distinguished by his innovative and creative approach. He's also the author of the book *The End of Religion*, which promotes a relational rather than a "religious" approach to faith and Jesus.

The other key thing about Bruxy is that he is unconventional, contemporary and fearless in his approach. He does not fit the stereotypical image of an evangelical pastor; first off, his appearance might scare and threaten some Christians, because with his shoulder-length hair and beard he actually looks like we think Jesus may have.

Probably more importantly, he is not afraid to "go there" in dealing with controversial subjects like wrestling with doubt, something a lot of pastors steer away from for fear of "spooking" their congregations.

"I was fortunate enough to be born into a home where I heard about Jesus from the very start. I first made a public confession of faith as a child in a children's service about at the age of five.

"And here's what's fascinating: I started doubting my own faith right there and then. I remember this vividly, going forward at an altar call at a children's service, receiving Jesus into my heart and praying a prayer with others, and then walking out of that service and saying, 'I feel new. I feel different. I feel better.' And then immediately following that saying, 'Yeah, but I'm young. What do I know? Maybe these emotions are just pretend.' And in my own kind of five-year-old brain I was already playing the role of Doubting Thomas. And ever since then, I have been Doubting Thomas, but the good news is, Doubting Thomas actually was a disciple of Jesus. He wasn't someone Jesus kicked out of the fold."

However, this would be a faith that would be strongly tested when his wife left him for another man and he went through an unexpected and devastating divorce.

"Very early in my ministry, my personal life collapsed in a way that was a complete shock to me. I didn't see it coming, and I still look back and I don't know why I didn't see it coming, but I didn't. My wife of many years rather rapidly left me for another man, divorced me, married him, had kids with him, built a new family, and this all happened fairly quickly. So it became evident that there was not going to be reconciliation. Now they were married and raising a family on their own, while I was still in shock and sorting out the pieces.

"Yeah. It left me unable to really recognize myself. If you were to ask me, 'Who are you, Bruxy? Describe yourself,' I would talk about my loving family. I would talk about my wife. If you asked me to describe my own abilities or who I was internally, one of the things on the list would be that I'm a pretty good judge of character. I read people well. I can anticipate things. So I was even left asking 'Who am I?' because I didn't read this situation well. I didn't see this coming, and what does that say about me? I didn't even seem to know myself then very well.

"You know, some people are left in a situation like that saying, 'I don't trust my former spouse' or maybe 'I don't trust that whole gender. I don't trust women. I don't trust men' or 'I don't trust relationships.' For me, I was left saying, 'I don't know if I can trust myself and my own abilities to even discern what's happening around me, since this was such a shock.'"

At the opening of this chapter we talked about comfort zones being collapsed brutally and cruelly. In Bruxy's case it was a cherished marriage and family life that ended suddenly and unhappily. The point in regard to *Trusting Through the Transition* is that we never know what tomorrow will bring and we must be ready, or as ready as it's possible to be.

So how did Bruxy move forward and cope with this very unhappy chain of events?

"Once again, just as I got into Christian ministry because of others in the church gathering around me, I was sustained through this the same way—by the power of community and God working through brothers and sisters in my life.

"Once again, spiritual brothers and sisters built me up and sustained me. So, in some sense, it was as the book says, 'the best of times and the worst of times.' It was the most devastating time in my life and yet the time when I saw the Church—meaning the community of faith—become one of the greatest strengtheners and sustaining powers in my life. I really fell in love once again with this idea of Jesus, of the Church, of Christian community.

"Well, instead of saying I don't trust people anymore, for me it was 'I have to trust more. I have to have around me people I can trust and who are discerning and who always live in community.' Married or single, no one should be on their own living as an island, and no marriage should operate as two people marooned on an island. I think the power of extended family and extended spiritual family is a real theme in the New Testament. So I fell in love all over again with the family of faith, the Church.

"Sometimes at points of crisis like this people are tempted to get bitter at God. My understanding is that God has created us in his image. And that means that he has created us to love. And that means that he has created us with free choice, because love necessitates a free choice. And that means that we can use our choice for good or evil, for building up or for tearing down. And so I believed it was a series of human decisions that led to this, and I wasn't going to blame God for it. In fact, I needed God more than ever.

"The other thing I do—and this is going to be a theme, I suppose, whenever talking about my life—is I turn to spiritually mature, God-loving brothers and sisters in the faith. And I surround myself with healthy relationships. I think the answer to broken relationships is not to withdraw yourself from relationships, but it is to connect yourself all the more with healthy and healing relationships.

"I think that there is a New Testament theme of brotherhood and sisterhood of those people who were Christ-followers where the apostle Paul would write to his friend Timothy and tell him to treat older women as mothers and younger women as sisters. And there's just this sense of family that is sometimes biological, sometimes purely spiritual, but always real and important to us.

"And I would encourage people at that level to make sure those relationships are strong. At their local church, however they experience church and express church, to make sure that they have very healthy brother and sister relationships that are pouring into them. It's almost like relationship multivitamins that you get in a relationship like that, which I think help build up your immune system so you don't become sick with mistrust."

I truly believe this is good and timely advice. We can't stop the storms of life, whether they be the financial variety or the more personal kind of family and relationship breakdown that Bruxy Cavey went through.

However, as we follow the Kingdom Promise of seeking first the kingdom, we also must remember that this is not meant to be a solitary pursuit. The purpose of the Church is to gather together as believers, because as Jesus said in Matthew, *"For where two or three are gathered together in My name, I am there in the midst of them"* (Matthew 18:20 NKJV).

Obviously this speaks to the literal power of communal Christian gatherings, but also, as in the quote at the beginning of this chapter from the second chapter of Acts, the first believers lived an existence of interdependence, sharing resources and property, eating, worshipping and living together for a common purpose.

Now as we know, they felt compelled to do this because they were struggling to literally survive against persecution and the perpetual threat of martyrdom. For the simple fact of the matter is that there's strength in numbers, and when the burden is heavy it's lighter when shared.

Remember, as in the Bulgarian proverb, God promised a safe landing, not an easy journey.

CHAPTER 13

Shooting Star

Paul Henderson

"Blessing I will bless you, and multiplying I will multiply your descendants as the stars of the heaven."

Genesis 22:17 NKJV

"Here's a shot! Henderson made a wild stab for it and fell. Here's another shot, right in front. They score! Henderson has scored for Canada!"

Canada-USSR hockey series,
Moscow, September 28, 1972

In this book we are focusing on how difficult circumstances or the threat of difficult circumstances can bring us closer to God. There is no doubt about it: crises and setbacks in our lives can have a silver lining. When our man-made plans fail, it can make us dig deeper to see what's missing.

Most of us are focused and even obsessed by our circumstances, whether we want to admit it or not. We tell ourselves if we only could change our specific situation our lives would be perfect. You know, "If I only could get that promotion or that raise, I'd have it made."

Or we play the blame game, laying the fault for our failings and short-comings on others, rightly or wrongly, as a means of exonerating ourselves. In an impending financial crisis, many of us will blame the world economic situation for our outcome, but that it is beside the point. What we are not recognizing is that salvation through Christ is not achieved because of our circumstances but in fact is achieved despite them.

As Gary Gregor, who's quoted earlier in this book, used to say in his role as a sports psychologist, "Winning teaches you nothing. It reinforces the illusion that you're perfect. It's losing that forces you to re-evaluate, and that tends to be where the growth comes from."

That's why the testimony of Paul Henderson is unique. He is a man whose spiritual growth came after he had accomplished one of the greatest feats in Canadian sports history in arguably the seminal moment in the legacy of our national sport, hockey.

On September 18, 1972, forty years ago, Henderson scored the goal in the waning moments of the first hockey series against Russia, the Summit Series, to secure both the game and the series for Canada. But there have been countless big hockey games and big goals. What is it that makes Henderson's so important?

At that time in the early 1970s the NHL was the pinnacle of professional hockey, with teams located across North America, and the players were almost exclusively Canadian. Amateur hockey and its elite events, the winter Olympics and the World Hockey Championships, were dominated by the Russians.

Russian players couldn't play in the NHL because they weren't allowed to leave Russia. The USSR was not only challenging us for hockey supremacy; they were our deadly rivals in a worldwide cold war of ideologies that always seemed to be heading dangerously towards an apocalyptic nuclear holocaust.

The odds and the implications were enormous. Canadians looked forward to the matches with a mixture of anticipation and dread. On one hand they dismissed the Russians, who routinely beat up on amateur squads, as all hype. Canada's players were no amateurs; this was the elite of the NHL, battle hardened pros who in our minds would make mincemeat of the less skilled Soviet challengers.

However, when the puck was dropped for the first game in Montreal at the legendary Forum, the entire nation was in for a giant shock. After Canada jumped out to a quick 2–0 lead, the Russians stormed back, putting on a jaw-dropping display of precision. Passing, skating and shooting at a dizzying pace, they seemed like a machine, almost robotic. They crushed the Canadians 7–3 and in the process made the NHL superstars look like an over-the-hill out-of-shape crew who were overwhelmed and struggling to keep up.

After five games the Russians had a three to one game lead with another game tied, which meant that Canada had to run the table by winning the three remaining games, all of which would be played in Moscow with Russian referees providing "home cooking" assistance to the home team cause.

But that was when Paul Henderson began his amazing run. At the time Henderson was an unlikely hero, a 29-year-old veteran, a solid if unspectacular player with Detroit and then the Toronto Maple Leafs. He made the Canadian team based on a career-best previous NHL season, scoring an impressive 38 goals for the Leafs. There were better known players on the team, like Bobby Orr (who actually didn't play because of injuries) and Phil Esposito of the Stanley Cup champion Boston Bruins, but it was Henderson who would emerge as the hero.

Henderson potted the game winners in both games 6 and 7 to tie the series, and then the magic moment occurred. With just 34 seconds left in the game, Henderson jumped on a rebound and put it past legendary Russian goalie Vladislov Tretiak for the biggest win in Canadian hockey history.

It was called "the goal heard around the world," and for Canadians who were old enough in 1972, it was a moment in time they will never forget. Like 9/11, the Kennedy assassination or the first landing on the moon, we remember where we were when it happened.

The impact on Henderson was overwhelming; he went from being a successful player to a national hero and superstar overnight. On the surface it must have seemed that things couldn't have been better, but that's not the reality of what faced Henderson when he returned to Canada and the NHL after the series.

"Fear can be a great motivator, and I was very afraid that I would be part of the team that lost to the Russians and be known as losers for the rest of our lives. Canada is not a big nation, but hockey is our game. Everyone on the team felt a responsibility to win. I had confidence that our team was better than the Russians, but it never entered my mind that it would be me that would score the winning goals in the last three games. It certainly gave me a stature that I would not have had without it. I wish I could have handled things much better and more maturely. If I'd had a spiritual dimension to my life at the time, I know I would have handled it more intelligently.

"In 1972, I had fulfilled most of my boyhood dreams, and I knew I was a very fortunate and blessed individual. Yet there was restlessness, a discontentment in the centre of my being, that I could not ignore. I was frustrated and disappointed. There were things about my life that I didn't know how to handle. Things were not going well with the Maple Leafs, the team I was playing on, and I was having major conflicts with the owner, Harold Ballard. Here I was playing in the NHL, doing something that I had always strived for, but I had become more discouraged than I had ever been in my life.

"I started drinking too much as a way to soothe the pain. I think if you are in a negative state of mind, you look for a way out. You get with the boys and you try to 'make merry,' but you wake up the next morning and it's there again.[1]

"Fortunately, Mel Stevens, who ran Teen Ranch near Orangeville, encouraged me to examine the claims of Jesus. He told me that I hadn't taken care of my soul and had never really looked at what it was on the inside. That made sense to me, so I started to read the Bible and wanted to understand who Jesus really was. Jesus claimed to be God, and he said he loved me and wanted me to know him, and the reward was eternal life."

It was a two-year search, spending hundreds of hours reading the Bible and other good books and meeting with Mel weekly. Henderson had to overcome his own built-in bias against Christianity, as he told Gary Gradley recently.

"It took me two years to surrender my life to the Lord because I was so skeptical about Christianity. I thought the people that can't make it in life had to turn to God, using Christianity as a crutch. I've always prided myself in being a self-made man, as I grew up poor and I did it all on my own. I woke up one day and finally realized and understood that nobody ever makes it on their own."

Because of some great mentoring by Mel Stevens and later John Bradford, Henderson went on to seminary, and in 1985 he started a men's ministry, now known as Leadership Impact Group. For the last 27 years he has dedicated his life to mentoring thousands of men, developing their leadership, the way he was mentored. After his career in hockey, Paul in his full-time ministry has used his immense celebrity status not to gain fame and fortune but to win souls for God.

"In the Bible, 1 Peter says as each one of us has received a special gift, employ it in serving one another as good stewards of the grace of God. And so God expects us to use what we've been given. I think several of my gifts are encouragement, exhortation and evangelism, and that is what I have been doing. I feel fulfilled when I'm doing this, and that's why I started the ministry. I've been working with men now for 27 years, encouraging them to get to know the Lord and then mentoring them and exhorting them to go deep and be all that God would ever want them to be.

"I find the greatest days of your life are the ones when you know you've enabled somebody else or encouraged them. So many times I'll pray every morning, 'Lord, if there's anybody that needs encouragement today, you bring them to my mind. Let me call them.' So many times I've phoned people and said, 'You know, I just felt that I should call you and pray for you today.' And so many times I hear people say, 'Boy, Paul, I needed that. I can't believe that you phoned me today.' I mean, that's awful satisfying, and you know that you're doing something worthwhile. I mean, scoring the goal in '72 was an incredible experience. There's no question about that, but when I look over my shoulder, when I've led people to Christ and helped them develop and become leaders and I see them making their lives count, the goal absolutely pales in significance."

Paul's purpose statement for decades has been to be a "godly world change agent" leading men to the Lord. Paul defines this unique term as follows: *Godly* means to live every day in a manner pleasing to and in obedience to God. *World* refers to using your profile and influence to have a vast impact on people around the globe. Finally, *change agent* means being able to transform lives in the same manner that godly men like Mel Stevens and John Bradford did for him years earlier, changing people's priorities, their thinking, their beliefs, and ultimately to bring them into a strong relationship with God.

For many, Paul Henderson is a man who has lived a "charmed" existence—a sports icon, a national hero and a giant of the faith, with a successful fifty-year marriage, three children and seven grandchildren. However, life has brought challenges for him, as for all of us. Paul is suffering from chronic lymphocytic leukemia.

"I was diagnosed with cancer in November of '09, and I've lived with cancer now for the last two and a half years. When you get cancer, and especially when you've taken care of yourself physically, it's a shock. I know God didn't give me cancer, but I know he's very aware of it. So, can I trust God now? And the reality is yes, I can, and the wonderful thing about it— I can say without question—I've had no fear or angst since I was diagnosed with cancer, and that is supernatural.

"I'm not that brave a person, but I've walked with the Lord now for 37 years and trust him implicitly because I've seen God be faithful time and time again. There have been all kinds of challenges along the way, but as each one comes I say, 'Okay, Lord, we've got a problem here.' I say, 'I need your help' and do ask for help every morning.

"I can honestly say the last two and a half years with cancer have been as good as any time I've ever had in my life. When you get cancer you can very quickly differentiate the trivial from the important, and the better you do that, the better you live."

The late artist Andy Warhol once said, "Everybody is going to be famous for 15 minutes." Well, Paul Henderson's "15 minutes" have lasted 40 years and counting. "The goal heard around the world" still resonates with Canadians; the jersey Henderson wore when he scored it was auctioned off in 2010 for an astounding 1.275 million dollars, an absolute record for a piece of hockey memorabilia.

Worldly celebrities appear like meteorites across the sky and burn out as quickly as they appear, but thousands of years ago Abraham formed a covenant with God in which the Lord promised to bless his descendants and multiply them like the stars in heaven. These stars don't burn out; they burn eternally.

"I believe my whole life has been a wonderful gift from God. Because of my faith and trust in him I'm totally convinced that I'm going to live for eternity. This life is not the game. This is just the warm-up for the game. The game is eternity in heaven with God.

"If I could have any one prayer answered, even over my own healing (and we pray for it every day), it would be that we would leave a legacy of an unbroken line of descendants who love Jesus until he returns."

[1] Paul Henderson and Roger Lajoie, *The Goal of My Life* (Toronto: Fenn-M&S, 2012).

Chapter 14

The Power of Prayer

Mike Gartner

"Therefore I say to you, whatever things you ask when you pray, believe that you receive them, and you will have them."

Mark 11:24, NKJV

This book is called *The Kingdom Promise*, which speaks to believers about the 1,260 promises God has made in his Word. But this also raises the question, "How do you activate these promises?"

The answer is simple: pray! *"Be anxious for nothing, but in everything by prayer and supplication, with thanksgiving, let your requests be made known to God"* (Philippians 4:6 NKJV).

The fact is, you don't have because you don't ask (James 4:2). There are two purposes to prayer, the first to praise and worship God and the second to specifically petition God. Now some might feel a little shy about aggressively lobbying God for their needs, but that's exactly what Jesus has instructed us to do.

Christ instructed us to not give up and to be persistent always, and he used the parable of the widow who constantly petitioned the judge. Although he was unrighteous, he eventually succumbed to her constant and unending lobbying. It also proves the principle that determination and constant vigilance will pay off.

Then He spoke a parable to them, that men always ought to pray and not lose heart, saying: "There was in a certain city a judge who did not fear God nor regard man. Now there was a widow in that city; and she came to him, saying, 'Get justice for me from my adversary.' And he would not for a while; but afterward he said within himself, 'Though I do not fear God nor regard man, yet because this widow troubles me I will avenge her, lest by her continual coming she weary me.'" Then the Lord said, "Hear what the unjust judge said. And shall God not avenge His own elect who cry out day and night to Him, though He bears long with them? I tell you that He will avenge them speedily. Nevertheless, when the Son of Man comes, will He really find faith on the earth?" (Luke 18:1–8 NKJV)

As a real life example of this we turn to Mike Gartner, an NHL star for 19 seasons and a member of the Hockey Hall of Fame. Early in his NHL career Gartner was brought to Christ by fellow Washington Capital teammate Jean Pronovost.

"Jean and I became really good friends. He was very successful as a right winger in the NHL, had scored 50 goals, which is a milestone. So I kind of looked up to Jean, and I was hoping that he could help me out in different parts of the game and show me the ropes, so to speak.

"Jean through a series of discussions asked if I wanted to go to a Bible study at his house, so a few of the guys from the team went over to his house and had a Bible study. I enjoyed it, and I enjoyed opening up the Word of God really for the first time and seeing what it had to say.

"I was confronted with the truth of the gospel of Jesus Christ, and I came to the point in my life where I had to make a decision. It really seemed that I was separated from God through the way I was living and through the sin that was in my life.

"It was not something where things were going poorly, because they weren't. I was having a good rookie season, and I was having a good second year in the league, and things were going very well.

"I wasn't looking for anything, but at that point I was confronted with the truth. I saw how Jean lived, and it was something that I really wanted for my life, and I made that decision. The truth for me was just overwhelming and the evidence was overwhelming, and I just felt I needed to make a decision, which I did. That was in the winter of 1981, and I've been following the Lord ever since."

However, as often happens, Mike soon was confronted by a major crisis that tested his new-found faith.

"I think it was my third year of pro; I got hit in the eye with a puck. I never wore eye protection and so I was hit directly in the eye with a puck. I lost my vision in my one eye for about two weeks, and when I went to the ophthalmologist he said that I had damage to the optic nerve behind my eye. He wasn't sure if it would heal or not. He had no way of knowing whether my eye would heal, and so I didn't know at that time. I couldn't even drive a car. I could barely see out of my one eye.

"It was painful too, but it was more painful when I found out that I couldn't see out of my one eye. I had one dominant eye anyway. My one eye has astigmatism in it, and I didn't see all that well out of it anyway. Then I had an eye that really dominated my eyesight, and that was the eye that got damaged, so I really couldn't see very well, not only out of the eye that was damaged but out of the other eye as well. I prayed at that time that God would heal my eye so I could continue to play and really just put it in his hands, not knowing whether I would continue to play hockey or not.

"So sure enough, after a couple of weeks it started to come around a little bit, and I started playing, even though my eyesight wasn't 100 per cent. I continued to pray, and I guess about three months later my eye finally got to the point where it was healed enough and I had a complete recovery from it. That was an early stage in my life and in my career when I really had to trust in God's plan and God's sovereignty."

The rest, as they say, is history. Not only did Mike recover and survive, he thrived. He is known as Mr. Consistency for his exceptional performance over an extended period of time. He has the NHL record for having posted an amazing seventeen 30-goal seasons and is tied with Jaromir Jagr with 15 consecutive 30-goal seasons. Clearly, God's grace has been at work in Mike Gartner's life for over three decades, and the results speak for themselves.

So the message is clear: your miracle is coming. Keep believing, keep praying and keep the faith!

"Without God, we cannot; without us, God will not" (St. Augustine).

Chapter 15

Obedience to God

Phil Geldart

"But why do you call Me 'Lord, Lord,' and not do the things which I say?"

Luke 6:46 NKJV

The purpose of this book is to strengthen believers as we prepare for difficult times, so we can not only survive but actually thrive no matter what our external circumstances are.

Obviously we believe that everything flows from Matthew 6:33, in that you must "*seek first the kingdom of God and His righteousness*" (NKJV).

So what is meant by this? Well, in a nutshell it means obeying God's commandments, seeking and listening to his guidance, and, as in Jesus' words from Luke 6, doing what you are told.

Reverend Bruce Smith has a great saying: "We demonstrate how much we love God by obeying him." This clarifies the opening Scripture of this chapter, where Jesus pointed out the corollary of this when he chastised the disciples for calling him Lord on one hand while disobeying him on the other. This is critical, because we will never receive God's blessings stored up for us unless we are obedient.

Dr. David Mainse is even more specific: "Faith is just obedience. That's all you need, enough faith to obey. Real faith—find out what the Word of God says; obey it. Find out what the still small voice says inside; go for it and believe in God for it."

In this context we turn to Phil Geldart, the founder and CEO of Eagle's Flight, Canada's largest corporate training and development company that specializes in experiential adult-based learning. For over 25 years Phil has been a faithfully obedient servant of the Lord, and God has blessed his business abundantly.

Phil, a strong and committed Christian, made a huge leap of faith to set up his company. He left his executive position with a large salary and a gold-plated benefit and pension package in order to front his own enterprise with personal monies and zero guarantees, with the huge risk that if it failed he could lose everything.

Phil is very strong on the issue of obedience: "I think that Christians misunderstand Scripture. There is the revealed will of God, which states that we first surrender our lives to him in obedience and second go into the entire world and preach the gospel. That is a command. The great commission is clear. Now how you execute that command is the intervention of God in your life. My calling is to be obedient to God."

As Phil says, "If God says to me, 'Go here and you'll be successful,' and I go and I'm successful, I'm not surprised. If I don't do what he says, of course I'm not going to be successful. So faith is not something I have or something additional to my ministry or my work; faith is why I am here.

"Our faith is demonstrated through our obedience. In my case it's to lead and run this company. I believe in the long run, this is where God wants me. Now the fact that at the end of the day I believe that God is going to deal with the financial is me living by faith based on what I believe he's going to do. But whether he does it or not is not a measure of the blessing of God. The blessing of God is in the relationship, not the manifestation.

"The question should be 'How is your faith causing you to be more intimate with God, causing you to love him more, causing you to use him more?'

"John 15:16 says, 'I've chosen you that you can go and bring forth fruit.' Not cars, not businesses, not shareholder value—fruit. If you get the shareholder value along the way, fine. Some are going to get it and some aren't.

"The fruit is people coming to Christ, people being godlier, people knowing the Word better, and people having a better relationship with God. God says, 'You've got a job to do, so just do what I tell you to do.' This was not my first choice, this is not what I signed up for, but this is where God wants me. It's very clear. So here I am. Welcome to my army.

"You go fight the battle. You go show people what it's like to be a Christian in the real world. We are called to be a light in a dark place. So every single day, I have got to live a Christian life in front of all these people and all these companies and all these executives.

"If you are obedient and you are where God wants you to be and it's tough, there are several promises that God is giving you even before you get on your knees. If I'm going to go do something as a servant of the living God, then I'd better go in the power of God. I trust God, I pray, I ask for guidance, I look to the Holy Spirit, and the Holy Spirit provides guidance.

"That's faith, that's living by faith.

"So you've got a company to run, a family to run, a school to teach, a classroom of students that you're working with. If you're a plumber repairing a pipe, it doesn't matter. If God says go, go. If God says don't go, don't go. I am a child of God, a sheep. He's the shepherd. It's not religion; it's a relationship."

Geldart goes on to describe how you take this faith and apply it in what you do your life. "What is God's plan for your life? What does God want for you? That's not the right question. The right question is, what does God want for himself? My life is, I'm a servant. God says, 'Listen, it's really clear. The plan I have for your life is that men and women will grow in godliness.' That's the plan that God has for Christians—period.

"'I want you to fight on the corporate battlefield.' But he could just as soon tomorrow say, 'I want you to go fight in Uganda.' All right, then I'll go to Uganda. So, the plan that God has for me is that I will be obedient to him. God says, 'I need you to go do what I need you to do.'

"The Bible says the steps of a good man are ordered by the Lord. So we have to take steps, and in the taking of the steps he directs those steps. So I go, 'OK, fine, I'm going to go do what you want me to do.' This is where he wants me to do battle. So I am doing battle. So when you say, 'What is the vision or the plan of God for your life?' it's to be obedient every day.

"But there are other plans for my life. God says, 'Be a responsible husband.' God says, 'Be a responsible father.' That's his plan. But when man says, 'What's your plan?' it's as if there's some blueprint. The blueprint is in the Word of God. It's to win the world for Christ. That's the blueprint. The vision is to win the world for Christ."

No one claims though that it is going to be easy, which is exactly what Geldart found out during the most recent recession. "Eagle's Flight has been the ultimate test of my faith, from April 2009 until about September of 2010. So when I am challenged, wondering if I am going to make the sales, if I am going to make payroll, I'm learning obedience because I've surrendered myself to the Holy Spirit. God provided the knowledge about how to lead and how to apply that knowledge. The confidence to lead in that fashion was because I knew I was where God wanted me. What people don't understand is that what they saw as the fruit of the tree, which is leadership and confidence, was rooted in faith nourished every single morning."

These are key points that Phil Geldart is making about obedience. Ask yourself, "How far am I prepared to go for God? What would I be willing to do? What would I sacrifice?" These are not easy questions, for as the Bible tells us almost all of the major prophets, Jesus' disciples and the apostles were martyred for their faith, so they literally gave all, as did he.

"God is going to cause you to grow. Even Jesus, his son, learned obedience through the trials that he suffered. Though he was a son, the son of God, perfect, incarnate, the creator of the universe came to this earth and learned through suffering. What did he learn? Obedience!" (Hebrews 5:8).

Chapter 16

Seventy Times Seven

John and Eloise Bergen

"For if you forgive men their trespasses, your heavenly Father will also forgive you. But if you do not forgive men their trespasses, neither will your Father forgive your trespasses."

Matthew 6:14–15 NKJV

Unforgiveness, the Bible tells us, is an absolute deal breaker with God, and it's deadly for us. Yet many hang on to old grudges and hurts as though they are a noble and worthy cause, and because of this they are bound to them.

Someone once described unforgiveness as where "you drink the poison hoping that the person that you're mad at will get sick and die." Studies have shown that unforgiveness *can* lead to disease and even death. Just google "unforgiveness and illness" and you will be amazed by how much medical research has been done on this very topic. It's clear that the stress, anger, hostility and despair caused by unforgiveness can destroy a person's health. Being in a state of unforgiveness over time can compromise your immune system, and that makes you vulnerable to a plethora of maladies, from heart disease to cancer.

So if not forgiving is so destructive, why do we cling so fervently to our resentments? Well, *forgive* is just a word, but forgiveness is an act that must come from the heart, and that can be hard. People don't forgive others when they feel the transgressions against them are heinous and by forgiving the offending party they somehow would let them off the hook.

We all would do well to consider the parable of the wicked servant and the lesson Jesus taught on the topic:

> *Then Peter came to Him and said, "Lord, how often shall my brother sin against me, and I forgive him? Up to seven times?" Jesus said to him, "I do not say to you, up to seven times, but up to seventy times seven."*
> (Matthew 18:21–22 NKJV)

So as well as making you literally sick, unforgiveness is a major obstacle in your relationship with God and his ability to bless you, and as we go through the transition of tough times, this isn't good.

So how do you put this in practice? Let's look at the story of John and Eloise Bergen. They are a retired couple from British Columbia who had travelled to Africa to do missionary work in Kenya.

Near tragedy struck one night in 2008 when a local gang inexplicably attacked them. First they went after 70-year-old John, beating both of his legs and breaking his arms and his jaw, slashing him with machetes numerous times and then leaving him for dead in the bushes.

Then they burst in on his wife, Eloise, 65, who was in the bathtub, and beat and slashed her with machetes as well. And then all three violently raped her.

Miraculously, Eloise had enough strength left to find John and then drive both of them to the hospital, where despite deep odds they both survived. They are now still recovering, but what is so compelling about this story is the reaction the Bergens had to their attackers, which is certainly not the way most of us would react.

"I can't wait for the day I can meet them and put my arms around them," said John right after the attack, referring to the men who had committed the crime, now incarcerated and awaiting trial.

Eloise spent time in her hospital bed in Kenya repeatedly saying the words "I forgive you." "I knew just in my mind that my words were important for my own ears to hear," she said. "If we don't forgive, it's like poison in our own systems."

Now ask yourself this: if people who were from the same area you had travelled to with the sole purpose of helping them attacked you, leaving you for dead like John, or beating and raping you like Eloise, could you find it in your heart to forgive them?

If we're honest with ourselves we will probably concede that this would be very tough to do. It's no accident that John and Eloise are committed

Christians who have dedicated their lives to helping the underprivileged and needy in places like Africa, and they put the teachings of their faith first.

Now this story as reported in the media across Canada is incredible enough, but what hasn't been reported in the years since this happened is even more inspiring.

In a recent conversation with John he told me that not only have he and Eloise been back to Kenya but they are working on building a new school in the very place that they were attacked.

In addition John purchased five acres in that area, and with the help of an American friend they have irrigated it and are now growing enough food crops to greatly assist in feeding the people, including 200 widows and children living there who without this kind of initiative would probably be starving.

Most amazing, John has visited the prison where the attackers are incarcerated and met with them face to face, forgiving them and sharing Christ with them, and they all prayed to receive Jesus as their Lord and Saviour.

Now this is true Christianity at work as Jesus envisioned it, and it shows the redemptive power and impact that forgiveness and grace can bring.

As it says in the book of Genesis, relating to the trials of Joseph and his deceitful brothers, *"But as for you, you meant evil against me; but God meant it for good, in order to bring it about as it is this day, to save many people alive"* (Genesis 50:20 NKJV).

They have written a book called *Forgiveness in the Face of Terror,* which can be ordered through their website, http://www.bergensmission.com.

So what is the key to being able to forgive? I think it's simple: obey your heavenly father, and he will do the rest. *"What is impossible with man is possible with God"* (Luke 18:27 NIV).

CHAPTER 17

"I Am the Vine": Staying Connected

Ron Ellis

"I am the vine, ye are the branches: He that abideth in me, and I in him, the same bringeth forth much fruit: for without me ye can do nothing."

John 15:5 KJV

As you know, kingdom living is not the same as worldly living. In fact, in many cases it is diametrically opposite.

And because of that, if we are to realize the Kingdom Promise and then, most importantly, apply it to receive the abundance promised us by Jesus, we must understand and be aware of these differences and how they affect us.

When we discuss kingdom principles, we talk of sowing and reaping and harvesting as the source of all existence and also the principle of successful living. This metaphor is extended by Jesus to describe him as the source or the "vine," and we are grafted in as branches of the vine, and thus we are totally dependent on the vine for both life and the ability to bear fruit.

Now this is where it gets interesting. The world advocates self-reliance and glorifies the "self-made" man or woman, whereby it's all about you and what you can accomplish without the intervention or assistance of anything or anyone. Therefore, the theory goes, when you have climbed to the top of the mountain, you will get all the credit and you won't owe anyone anything.

This philosophy of self-reliance is the complete opposite of kingdom living. John Arnott, who is the founder and president of Catch the Fire

Ministry in Toronto, formerly known as the Toronto Airport Christian Fellowship, has a great little story that exemplifies this as a means of keeping him humble about the incredibly successful ministry he and his wife have built, in case they ever get confused about who the real star of the show is.

"There was a little donkey going in and out of Jerusalem, and one day he comes back, and he's all pumped up and full of pride. His mother says, 'What's with you?' He says, 'Oh Mom, today was an amazing day.' He says, 'I went into town. Everybody's taking their coats off, throwing them in front of me. They're waving palm branches. They're all yelling, "Hosanna." Man, am I ever special!' And his mother says, 'I hate to burst your balloon, but it wasn't you they were exalting. It was the one you were carrying.'"

In kingdom living, the metaphor of the vine, with Jesus being the vine itself and us being the branches, stands in stark contrast to this philosophy. His point is that "Because you are grafted into me, I feed you, and because of this you, the branch, bears fruit, just as the branch of the apple or pear tree does. However, conversely, if you are severed from me through disobedience, sin or disbelief, you are not connected to the vine, and thus it will be impossible for you to bear fruit, and thus your life will be barren."

Jesus was adamant about this to the disciples and even stated, "*Without Me you can do nothing*" (John 15:5 NKJV).

I raise this point because I believe many Christians have not captured this and are prone to adapt the "self-reliance" model of the world with a "value added" quality of being a Christian as a supplementary rather than a primary focus.

To illustrate this we turn to Ron Ellis. Ron was an integral part of the 1967 Stanley Cup winning club. Unfortunately, this was the last Stanley Cup winning team in Toronto, which makes it 45 years and counting.

In addition to his illustrious NHL career Ron, like Paul Henderson, was a member of Team Canada '72 that triumphed over the Russians. He played on the same line as Paul and Philadelphia's Bobby Clarke, and they led the way to Canada's legendary come-from-behind win.

However, like Paul, in the aftermath of this massive victory he began looking for something deeper in his life.

"You're going to see that Paul and I had very similar journeys to becoming Christians. After 1972 I think both of us began to really search for something that was missing in our lives, mainly because from a hockey perspective, what more could we have accomplished?

"Even a few years prior to 1972 in the Summit Series, Paul and I and our two roommates with the Leafs started to attend church on Sundays when we were on the road. And it was almost like the Lord had his hand on us and was trying to get our attention. For example, when we were in New York City, Norman Vincent Peale was preaching. We would get an opportunity to hear him.

"It's interesting to me why that became important to us. We were not Christians at the time. And after the '72 series was all over I think we both started to question what the real meaning of life is. Even though we accomplished probably the summit of our careers, there was certainly something missing.

"You've talked to Paul about Mel Stevens and Teen Ranch, and that certainly had an impact on me as well. Paul and I were both on the Leaf team when Mel presented Bibles to the team. And that resulted in an athletes' retreat at Teen Ranch in the month of July.

"Paul had become a Christian at that time. He had worked very closely with Mel, and Mel helped him answer a lot of questions. Paul put a little pressure on my wife and I to attend this retreat—we weren't Christians. And I reluctantly went. I still thought I was my own man, that I could do my own thing, but I'm so happy I went.

"Jan and I met Christian couples, athletes from various sports, professional athletes, and it wasn't long before we realized that these people had something that we didn't have that we felt we should have in our lives. It wasn't very long after that, within a couple of weeks, that my wife and I both invited the Lord into our lives."

However, life is not always simple, and in 1986 after his hockey career had ended Ron was diagnosed with clinical depression.

"I think we're tested on a daily basis, because we are not perfect. And we won't be perfect until we are with him, but certainly there was a point in my life that was very dark. I developed a serious bout of depression, and it lasted for quite some time.

"I had retired from the game of hockey for two years and then made a comeback. I know now that depression had its hands on me at that point. I didn't know what it was, I couldn't identify it, but I know now, as I learned so much about it. That's what was going on in my life at the time.

"I must admit I asked that question a lot of people ask when they face adversity as Christians: 'Why me? I mean, I'm trying to be a good Christian, I'm trying to attend church, I'm trying to help others. Why me, Lord?' That was something I had to deal with, and of course my faith was shaken.

"Fortunately, I had wonderful mentors. Mel Stevens comes to mind very quickly. He is my spiritual mentor. He helped me through this process. Other people of course were praying for me, and thankfully when I got over my pride and asked for help I was able to get the proper help.

"It wasn't an easy process. I think there's many characters in the Bible who went through this process as well, and it was not easy. You just have to get to a point where you can say, 'I don't understand all of this, but Lord, I just have to trust that you know what you're doing.' I had to yoke myself to him and just allow him to walk beside me and not try to pull on the yoke. That only creates more problems because they're man-made solutions, trying to pull him into an area where he doesn't want to be.

"It didn't happen overnight. I had to finally say to myself, 'I can't do this on my own.' I got to that point, and I said, 'OK, Lord, up to now we've had a pretty warm, fuzzy relationship, but this is where the rubber meets the road. I really have to trust you.'"

Ron's story is a perfect example of what Jesus was talking about in John 15:5. As a high profile NHL hockey star, he was seen as the embodiment of the self-made man, but he and his wife made a major commitment to give their lives to Christ at the height of his career. This couldn't have been easy, as generally the hockey world has been a stronghold of secularism, and many in that circle see Christians as weak and out of step with the "macho" lifestyle of an NHL warrior. However, it proved to be the best decision Ron ever made when after his career the dark clouds of depression surrounded him and he was facing a vicious adversary. Ron makes it clear it was his faith and relationship with Christ that pulled him through.

Today, Ron uses this experience to help others who are facing this very serious challenge. He speaks across Canada as an advocate for mental health, using his celebrity status and amazing testimony to raise awareness of an issue that almost every Canadian family has had to deal with but that also sadly seems to still carry a stigma.

Ron is connected to the "vine" of Jesus, and because of this he has been through the fire and come through victorious.

To read more about Ron, check out his excellent autobiography, *Over The Boards: The Ron Ellis Story* (Bolton, Ontario: Fenn Publishing, 2002).

CHAPTER 18

Rebuilding The Walls

Lorna Dueck

"You see the distress that we are in, how Jerusalem lies waste, and its gates are burned with fire. Come and let us build the wall of Jerusalem."

Nehemiah 2:17 NKJV

It is almost 6:00 on a Monday evening in the heart of downtown Toronto. Christian journalist Lorna Dueck stands before a live audience who have poured into a studio in the broadcast headquarters and mothership of CBC. Sitting in the same room where such Canadian cultural staples as "Hockey Night in Canada" and "The Rick Mercer Report" are broadcast, this crowd is here to view a taping marathon of "Context with Lorna Dueck."

The audience is about to witness this pillar of Christian media in Canada deftly work her way through three shows, with three guests each, exploring and digging deep into the news. They will watch as Lorna sifts through facts, presents a range of viewpoints and empowers each guest to share their unique insights, all towards the goal of exploring news and current affairs from a Christian worldview.

This is a Christian television show like no other, presented by a journalist passionate to find God's truth in each story she investigates.

The three shows taped on this night—after editorial nipping and tucking—will run across North America on 8 television networks, reaching viewers who will be challenged to recognize that God is indeed present, even in the most unlikely of stories.

What viewers particularly appreciate about Lorna, explains Director of Development Jeff Groenewald, are the moments when she is clearly veering off the script and the questions prepared beforehand by her able team, and following her own instinct to where the story is leading.

Moving off script—and away from predictability and safety—is a Dueck speciality.

It is what launched her from the security and quiet anonymity of a newspaper reporter in 1994 to front and centre on the iconic Christian show *100 Huntley Street*, co-hosting with veteran broadcaster David Mainse. "The character that required, the transparency that required, was probably my greatest faith challenge," says Lorna. "I went from being a layperson to being a Christian broadcaster on national television."

For a self-described introvert to operate on full steam extrovert mode day after day—and live on television—required a stretching of gifts and spirit. "I love to be quiet and read and think and study. So being a public person doesn't come naturally for me at all. To be on live daily national television, transparent about my Christian faith, was a big stretch for me," says Lorna. "Feeling out of control because it was a spontaneous television experience when I was primarily a print journalist. Print means you can lovingly nurture every word, instead of live TV, where you chat and extrapolate and react to the story happening in front of you. Those things really stretched me."

Even as Lorna was being stretched, the overwhelming response of viewers energized and moved her. She was being schooled in the power of media and, of course, God's power to work through it to reach Canadians.

"I was compelled as I watched the phone ring 1,000-plus times a day, as it did at *100 Huntley Street*. People were calling that number on the bottom of the screen to ask for prayer, salvation, hope, any number of things. I still love that show and the folks who work there. The Mainse family and their key staff were amazing mentors to me," says Lorna. "The audience need and interest was huge. It was very powerful to me to be a steward of that."

The memory of audience need and God's ability to meet those needs through interactive, cutting-edge media remained and grew with Lorna as she took a break from TV ministry to spend more time with her growing teenagers in 2004.

And it would be teenagers—and an encounter with them—that would propel Lorna's next big step of faith: moving the media ministry she created (after her own teens were launched) from the safety of familiar surroundings to the heart of Canada's broadcast empire, CBC.

"I was walking along on a windy day, and I saw eight blocks of teenagers lined up waiting for a wristband to watch the MuchMusic Awards," remembers Lorna. As a lover of Toronto history, Lorna knew that the Wesley building that houses MuchMusic's studio actually began as the publishing house of the Methodist Church, and later headquarters for the United Church of Canada. "It is where Canada's Bibles used to be published. And over the years since, that Christian media presence in creating Canadian culture has steadily been eroded. Today that Wesley Building, named for revivalist John Wesley, produces some of the most powerful television in the country. But not a word of it is about Christian instruction."

A long, winding line-up of youth eager to watch MuchMusic's big event—milling around a building still adorned with sculpted sheaves of wheat and books—had a deep and unexpected impact on Lorna. "As I contrasted the line-up of youth with the goals of the original building, the Lord just started to really speak to me that he wanted his presence back in the downtown media core of Toronto," she says.

"That was a very profound encounter, and I started to cry on the street. I felt God say, 'You need to move the media ministry to downtown Toronto.'" Around the same time, a CBC executive approached Lorna's team and encouraged them to try and get a lease in their downtown headquarters. "Our board of directors was all over that," says Lorna. "It was not exactly a practical move; it was a strategic plan to regain cultural influence for Christianity, and we had a unanimous vote to go for it. That began the next chapter—we launched a 30-day campaign to secure financing for a five-year lease and to build a beautiful office, right on the main floor of the CBC."

The team raised $1.8 million dollars in thirty days. "Those gifts became for me my pillar of fire, leading me through the wilderness, and I so needed that," says Lorna. "The fruit of that 30-day campaign made me just keep saying, 'God brought you here. This wasn't you. This wasn't your own idea. This is the Holy Spirit that is asking for a missionary presence in the CBC building and media culture in Canada. So stand and stand with it,'" she explains.

Today, Lorna stands in a CBC studio creating a show that is intelligent, provocative, and proof-positive that Christians have a role to play in Canada's media culture. In year two of their move downtown, Media Voice Generation, Lorna's umbrella ministry that produces the show, launched *Love Is Moving*, a brand new TV series aimed at youth.

Lorna continues to coordinate a monthly multi-faith online panel and write a column for national newspaper *The Globe and Mail* (www.globeandmail.com). The controversial column mixes opinion with politics, all from a faith perspective. A column that specifically considers the role of faith in politics for example—with Prime Minister Stephen Harper as the focus—garnered 500 online comments, many of them combative.

But Lorna is used to people not agreeing with her. The studious introvert who moved full-on into the public arena shed any remaining thin skin years ago. The journalist who friends describe as a modest, down-to-earth Christian wife, mother and working woman can hold her own on Canada's national stage. After all, she is an explorer of stories who sometimes finds herself being the story itself, as in a *Ryerson Review of Journalism* article that uses Lorna's work as a case-study to question if people of faith can be neutral in their reporting. Lorna's fearless answer to that question is in the article: "I don't think I'm neutral," she says. "I think I'm looking very specifically for a Christian angle."

That answer is part of the obedience that has driven Lorna's ministry. "I think God needs obedient people. If you totally believe in a project, I don't think that it's always going to come out the way you believe it. Rather, I believe God is sovereign and God is in control and I need to be a little bit loose and fluid with ideas," she says. "James 3:13-19 describes God asking us to be wise about our good deeds. And that wisdom in James does not describe the person who stands firm and resolute and says it will be this way or not at all. That wisdom describes a person who is peacemaker, who's listening, who gives in, who bends, all kinds of challenging things in that type of godly wisdom."

If there is a Bible character that is a parallel for Lorna Dueck, it must be Nehemiah, that Old Testament leader who shows up in the aftermath of the Babylonian invasion, called by God to return to Jerusalem and rebuild the walls of a city destroyed and in chaos.

But of course, the rebuilding was about more than mortar and walls. For Lorna it's a story about God's generosity to a populace who needed to find their spiritual home. It's about the determined teamwork, divine counsel and perseverance that can establish the love of God as a known fact in the media landscape.

(*To find out more about Lorna Dueck and* Context *please visit* www.contextwithlornadueck.com.)

CHAPTER 19

Sowing and Reaping

Bruce Smith

"Then Isaac sowed in that land, and reaped in the same year a hundredfold; and the LORD blessed him."

Genesis 26:12 NKJV

In kingdom living everything is based on sowing and reaping. If you want to reap much you must sow much, and he who sows little reaps little. This is a fundamental law of how the kingdom works and vital for us to both understand and practice if we are to realize God's blessings.

As a practical modern-day example of the power of sowing and reaping we turn to Reverend Bruce Smith, a former CFL Grey Cup winner and captain of the Toronto Argonauts. After his playing days he went on to become a super success in real estate, but then he moved on to his third and most important career, as an ordained minister and chaplain with King Bay Chaplaincy in Toronto.

Now that's quite an unusual progression. Bruce tells us what happened that prompted such a dramatic change.

"I was at this motivational seminar. You know how it's all rah-rah stuff. But it came to a point in the seminar where they got a piece of paper and asked, 'If you could have anything in your life, what would that be?' And for the first time in my life I stopped to do an evaluation of my life. I did an inventory of all my accomplishments: my Grey Cup ring, all my accolades in real estate, all my money, all my cars, all my watches, all my travelling, my full length otter fur coat, big line of credit, all that stuff. So when I finally got through with that, I looked at the other side, and of course it was blank, and so I said, 'Bruce, what is the one thing in life you want that you don't have?' I heard it clearly: 'You don't have peace. You've got no peace.'"

That led to a spiritual search, including sampling New Age and Eastern philosophies, but he then started going to church, and finally he committed his heart to Christ. It was a homecoming like the Prodigal Son in Jesus' parable in the book of Luke, because he was raised by a very strong Christian mother in Texas.

"I made a personal decision for Christ, and then of course, I got really emerged in going to church. Shortly after that, I got really emerged in reading the Bible. So on New Year's Eve 1994, going into 1995, I made a public confession and got baptized."

Bruce understands that kingdom giving is a covenant relationship with God, that when we give we have an expectation of receiving a "harvest" back in return. This was demonstrated a number of years ago when he "sowed" into a potential television ministry.

"About five years after becoming a Christian I had my first experience with kingdom living. I was invited to speak at a Christian business luncheon. They asked me to share my journey of faith. I met a businessman there, and shortly thereafter I met him again at a Bible study. The leader asked me to close the meeting in prayer, and he was really moved by my prayer.

"As we were leaving he said to me, 'Bruce you should have your own television show.' He went as far as calling several large ministries in the US to ask how to get someone on TV. They all said, 'Go to *100 Huntley Street*, and they will tell you what to do.'

"So we went and we shared our concept with the president of *100 Huntley Street*, and he encouraged us to move forward with the idea. He told us the cost of producing and airing the show. It was way more than what we thought it would be, so we were somewhat discouraged. I was attending a large Pentecostal church in Toronto, and at the Sunday service the pastor came to the pulpit and was very excited. He said that the church was going on television, and he encouraged the congregation to give a special offering for the new venture.

"Without any hesitation I decided to follow the kingdom way by sowing a seed for their show, with the expectation of receiving a 100-fold return for our show. That must have been a special seed, because the 100-fold return came quickly.

"I had a meeting with a businessman to share the vision for our show. As we were leaving he said he would like to sow the first seed toward our show. He wrote me a check for 100 times what I had sowed, which was enough to produce the show. However it wasn't enough to buy air time, but someone put us in touch with a producer who had just left *100 Huntley Street* to start his own production studio. He was able to help us create and produce the show for half the cost of the other studio, so we had enough for air time."

Those who know Bruce are not surprised by his remarkable show of faith. He is a spiritual giant, a large, gregarious man who loves God and Jesus and who now is wreaking havoc on the kingdom of darkness in the same way he once did as an all-star defensive lineman on opposing CFL quarterbacks.

"People just need to start trusting. God commended the widow because she gave two mites as an offering. She gave all she had. The rich folks gave only a little of what they had. He didn't commend them. He commended her, because she trusted. And that guaranteed her place in the kingdom." *"Assuredly, I say to you that this poor widow has put in more than all those who have given to the treasury; for they all put in out of their abundance, but she out of her poverty put in all that she had, her whole livelihood"* (Mark 12:43-44 NKJV).

"Over a period of time, I see that God is a giver. The whole law of reciprocity is the law of sowing and reaping. God is a giver. He gave his Son. So the more we serve and give, the more we become like God. You can never out-give God."

"Jesus says that the kingdom of heaven (God's way of doing things) is based on this fundamental principle. For example, God sowed his Son Jesus and has already reaped over two billion sons and daughter in return at this point. So if you have a need, sow a seed in the area of the need, just like I did. In other words, if you need money, sow money; if you want a trip, sow a seed to someone you know who wants to take a trip.

"The Word says that God gives seed to the sower. Therefore if you don't have a seed, ask God for it. However, when you get it, don't eat it. Sow it. When the harvest returns to you, if it's not enough to meet the need, sow it as another seed until you get what you need." *"Now he who supplies seed to the sower and bread for food will also supply and increase your store of seed and will enlarge the harvest of your righteousness"* (2 Corinthians 9:10 NIV).

CHAPTER 20

"Pressed Down, Shaken Together, and Running Over"

Annmarie Morais

"Give, and it will be given to you: good measure, pressed down, shaken together, and running over will be put into your bosom."

Luke 6:38 NKJV

This is a book about a promise that Jesus makes: when we seek God first, our worldly needs will be met.

However, as we also have seen in these testimonies, God will put us to the test to see whether we really are ready to step out in faith. Clearly the people in this book have taken the test and passed it with flying colours.

However, that doesn't mean that it's easy for any of us to put it all on the line in faith, particularly when resources are scarce.

A great example of this is Annmarie Morais, a brilliant young Canadian screenwriter. She was the first Canadian winner of the prestigious Nicholl Fellowship for Screenwriting, which is administered by the Academy of Motion Pictures Arts and Sciences (the same folks who organize a little annual awards show called the Oscars).

She has gone on to professional screenwriting success, including her original and highly successful feature *How She Move* and adapting the popular play *Da Kink in My Hair* for television.

This all sounds very glamorous—winning international awards, writing feature films, living in Hollywood, the mecca of the entertainment industry. However, there's a lot more to Annmarie's story and how her faith got her where she is today.

"I grew up in the Church, a teenager in the era where the wickedness of movie theaters (or more specifically the films that played in them) was preached from the pulpits. While I was a particularly obedient child, this was an area of secret non-compliance. I loved the magic of sitting in a dark theatre and letting a story sweep you away. I still do.

"I can only imagine the frustration of my practical West Indian parents to have all four of their children saddled with these 'impractical' artistic giftings, and their subsequent terror as their youngest child and only daughter trotted off to film school to try and turn a childhood knack for storytelling into a career.

"The decision had been met with a lukewarm reception from most of my childhood church family as Bible college was thought to be the godly choice for young men and women of that day. I can still remember the stinging words of a dear church mother after learning of my career plans: 'Christians have no place in the movie business!' It was a devastating declaration, but I could only reply with the answer that God had placed in my spirit long ago, that my gifts were not haphazardly given but requirements of my calling, and he was calling me to the entertainment industry.

"Four exhausting years and one very expensive film degree later, the sound of that call seemed faint in comparison to the other noises screaming in my ear. 'You're a film school graduate with half a dozen jobs and not one of them in film—what are you doing with your life?' My brilliant plan to pursue any job that would afford me the time to write screenplays seemed far less ingenious as my list of rejected scripts grew longer than my resume (and my patience). I had always been told, 'Where God guides he provides,' but my bank account begged to differ as negative balances became a commonplace occurrence.

"As months stretched into years, the dream of a screenwriter's life in Hollywood seemed as far as Hollywood itself from my basement apartment in Toronto.

"Sometime later a dear friend, also an aspiring writer, clued me into writing competitions for screenwriters. There were several available to writers like me living outside of America, but one stood as the 'holy grail,' if you will, above all others. This particular competition had the distinction of being associated with the Academy of Motion Picture Arts and Sciences…yes, the Oscar people. If you ever rehearsed an Oscar acceptance speech in the mirror (and who hasn't, really), you know what that little gold man means. I decided then and there that I would enter.

"The first year of submission met with no success, but in a competition that drew thousands of applicants from across the globe that was hardly a surprise. The next year, two of those jobs on my endless resume would play a pivotal part in the script I would submit. The first was from pre-university days in my hometown hospital where I had been struck by the incredible sweetness and sadness of a young woman, whose struggle with cutting (self-mutilation) became a source of inspiration for my story's heroine. Later, a job where a co-worker read my pages during lunch breaks and gave me her unabashed critique helped me reshape the drama to a finer point. I submitted the script and made the first round and the next, and then...the beige envelope arrived with the gold Oscar statuette embossed in the corner. I was in the finals. This was it!

"I must have screamed a million 'Thank you, Lords' and ran around the basement apartment like a mad woman. Even my boss was certain she'd be losing an employee to Hollywood when the judging committee selected the final five to receive a $25,000 fellowship. I had sent off all the required paperwork, including my letter to the committee explaining what I would write next if they granted me the fellowship, already on a mental shopping spree that began somewhere in Beverly Hills.

"A few weeks later, the long awaited phone call arrived while I was at work. The program administrator broke the news...I had not been selected for a fellowship. I didn't have to say a word to my boss hanging up the phone; she read my devastation and was equally emotional as she told me to go home early.

"It was as painful as it was bewildering. Why had God brought me so far only to slam the door? Why was my God of plenty letting me live in the land of lack when prosperity was within reach? There were no answers coming as I cried out in prayer, but even in the midst of sorrow came a certainty that I was still doing what he called me to do.

"My 'starving artist' status became something of a cautionary tale it seemed, and when a cousin told my aunt he wanted to pursue the arts and asked what it was I was doing, her horrified reply was 'She's starving, that's what she's doing!' My 'almost' win was not without its benefits though. I found literary representation and took a trip to Hollywood to see some important industry folks. Even a trip to the fellowship office proved fruitful as the sweet receptionist offered me encouragement, assuring me that my script lost out by a hair and I should re-enter it. It was all well and good, but it did not change the fact that I was as broke stepping off the plane back home as I had been stepping on.

"With plans to spend a few months in Los Angeles to see what might unfold, I attended a Sunday night service at my home church in Toronto. That evening Dr. Nasir Siddiki spoke about the seed and the harvest. Now if you've grown up in church as I have, this isn't an unfamiliar notion…you cannot expect to reap blessings if you do not first sow into the kingdom. I know that sowing isn't always financial—it may be investing your time, your talents or your encouragement into an area as God directs—but as Dr. Siddiki continued to speak I knew that what God was asking me to sow was what I was certain I didn't have to give…my money.

"When you're living life on a micro-budget every last penny is precious, and I had 15 dollars to my name. It was bus fare, it was food, it was gas, and it was all I had! I began to play the believers' bartering game with God (you know the one): 'Lord, if I just give a few dollars, that'd be good, right?' 'Lord, I wrote the Christmas and Easter productions; that was some serious talent and time sowing, wasn't it?' 'Lord…?' I weighed the certainty of what he was speaking to me against the reality of my circumstances, and it just wasn't adding up. While many around me were sowing large financial seeds in faith for large financial needs, my 15-dollar faith offering seemed almost laughable in comparison.

"In that same instant the Lord brought back the Bible story of the widow's mite in Mark 12. The amount was not as important as the offering. It was (and is) my desire to be a believer who operates on the 'You say, I obey' principle with God. It wasn't that he was asking for my last 15 dollars; he was asking for my obedience. In that understanding, the sowing came easy. Whatever my desires for success were, in that moment my desire for becoming the woman of God I was purposed to be was greater.

"If this was a fairy tale I would now tell you how life was all rainbows and candy after that moment, but the struggles did not evaporate. Still, a body of believers who spoke life and possibility to me at every turn surrounded me. There were also Sunday morning 'giving ninjas' who'd quickly slip a few dollars into my pocket when my head was turned. Doors of opportunity began to creak open, and, taking the advice of that sweet receptionist in the Los Angeles fellowship office, I resubmitted my same script with almost no changes. The script advanced and advanced, until the beige envelope with the gold Oscar arrived once more.

"My excitement to be a finalist was a little more muted this time around. Though I had beaten thousands to this place, the odds among the few remaining were not in my favour. No Canadian had ever won the coveted prize. No one had ever won with a resubmitted script, and to top it all off I had taken none of the script critiques (given in an unheard of gesture of kindness) by one of the Oscar-winning panel judges.

"When the administrator's call came, the 'Congratulations' nearly buckled my knees. I had won a fellowship, $25,000, and a small place in history, if not a tremendous step in my career.

"Looking back I can see God's hand in every twist and turn of the road. My understanding of the importance of sowing as an expression of love and not 'loss' was cemented in a moment of giving, and while I am grateful for the fiscal blessing it yielded I am most thankful for the mile-marker of faith God erected in my life before that harvest came.

"More than ten years later as I continue to ride the rollercoaster that is working life in the entertainment industry, I've experienced some incredible highs to be sure, but in those low 'valley' moments I look back on markers like this and others that declare the faithfulness of a Father I don't always understand but know I can trust with everything I have, even my dreams."

Annmarie Morais, a young artist, was so near and yet so far from a coveted career in the movie business. Down to her last 15 dollars, which she desperately needed for essentials, she gave it all in faith. The harvest was huge, just as the Lord said in his Word it will be if we give to him.

"'Test me in this,' says the LORD Almighty, 'and see if I will not throw open the floodgates of heaven and pour out so much blessing that there will not be room enough to store it'" (Malachi 3:10 NIV).

CHAPTER 21

The Wisdom of Solomon

Tim Cestnick

"King Solomon surpassed all the kings of the earth in riches and wisdom."

1 Kings 10:23 NKJV

If we are entering a period of real peril economically and a challenging future, isn't it time to examine the life of the richest man who ever lived, King Solomon, the former king of Israel?

As the heir to his father King David's throne, Solomon presided over an empire that was without comparison in the earthly realm. Not only was he the most powerful monarch on the face of the earth, he was the king of Israel who fulfilled his father's dream of building the temple in Jerusalem, the greatest shrine erected in the history of man and the place that housed the ark of the covenant, which contained the sacred stone tablets etched with the Ten Commandments.

Most of us would assume that as a person of noble birth Solomon would imperiously ask God to lavish great treasures and luxury upon him (and maybe demand it in the arrogant way that some of today's moguls conduct themselves). Once again we see the recurring theme: Solomon did not acquire great wealth, health and fruitfulness by seeking them directly but as a by-product of his search for wisdom.

This wisdom has been handed down to us today in the book of Proverbs in the Old Testament. It's important to see how through seeking righteousness we can attract all the things we need and desire in life:

Trust in the LORD with all your heart, And lean not on your own under-standing; In all your ways acknowledge Him, And He shall direct your paths. Do not be wise in your own eyes; Fear the LORD and depart from evil. It will be health to your flesh, And strength to your bones. Honor the LORD with your possessions, And with the firstfruits of all your increase; So your barns will be filled with plenty, And your vats will overflow with new wine. My son, do not despise the chastening of the LORD, Nor detest His correc-tion; For whom the LORD loves He corrects, Just as a father the son in whom he delights. Happy is the man who finds wisdom, And the man who gains understanding; For her proceeds are better than the profits of silver, And her gain than fine gold. She is more precious than rubies, And all the things you may desire cannot compare with her. (Proverbs 3:5–15 NKJV)

What we see in this excerpt from Proverbs is basically a confirmation of kingdom principles, or the kingdom secret itself.

Solomon has told us to seek God for everything (seek ye the king-dom) and to closely follow his commandments (seek ye his righteous-ness), and in so doing all the things that we need and seek—health, wealth and happiness—will be added unto us.

He reminds us of the tithe and first fruit offerings and their impor-tance. But probably most significant is that Solomon became an instru-ment or vessel for the wisdom of God. Solomon, the young king, did not have such wisdom; in fact he described himself in 1 Kings 3:7 as "*a little child*" who did not know how to go out or come in.

However, he was given the wisdom he needed for the massive task of ruling Israel through his obedience and surrender to God, and thus he "attracted" wealth, prosperity, health and fruitfulness.

In the book of Proverbs, Solomon expanded on his wisdom and gave us words to live by, which are principles we ignore at our peril. As we approach tough times, what advice has he given that are words to live by for the 21st century?

Obey and follow God: "*The fear of the LORD is the beginning of knowledge, But fools despise wisdom and instruction*" (Proverbs 1:7 NKJV).

Avoid debt: "*The rich rules over the poor, And the borrower is servant to the lender*" (Proverbs 22:7 NKJV).

Work hard to succeed: "*In all labor there is profit, But idle chatter leads only to poverty*" (Proverbs 14:23 NKJV).

Seek out and follow wise counsel: "*Where there is no counsel, the people fall; But in the multitude of counselors there is safety*" (Proverbs 11:14 NKJV).

Be honest and display godly integrity: *"Honest weights and scales are the LORD's; All the weights in the bag are His work"* (Proverbs 16:11 NKJV).

Do not chase after material things: *"Do not overwork to be rich; Because of your own understanding, cease!"* (Proverbs 23:4 NKJV).

Seek positive associations in your relationships with others: *"He who walks with wise men will be wise, But the companion of fools will be destroyed"* (Proverbs 13:20 NKJV).

Do not live an excessive lifestyle: *"The fear of the LORD prolongs days, But the years of the wicked will be shortened"* (Proverbs 10:27 NKJV).

Tim Cestnick, whom we introduced earlier as one of Canada's most respected tax and personal finance experts, is a modern-day dispenser of wisdom. Most importantly, Tim is a committed Christian. With his incredible accomplishments and talents, one would think he would be committed to building his personal empire, but such is not the case. He has his eyes on loftier goals.

"I have felt, for a long, long time, that one of my purposes, maybe my key purpose, is to give back financially. We often talk in church about how some people are 'senders' and some people are 'goers.' I think of myself as being responsible for not only sharing what God has done in my life—that is, the good news of the gospel—as the opportunity arises but also giving back financially and helping mobilize financial resources for God's work. That's where I get my greatest joy. It just feeds on itself. As I do things that I feel are right where God wants me to be, I get that real satisfaction, career satisfaction, and joy in what I do day to day; that's where I'm at.

"As I work with affluent families and speak to them about their strategic philanthropy and their wealth and what they are doing with it, I feel privileged all the time. The majority of these families have a real desire to give back and make a difference. They come to us for guidance in making their philanthropy more meaningful, and I gain a real joy knowing that I'm having a positive impact on them and their wealth. It's a tremendous opportunity to help guide significant resources in purposeful ways."

Tim Cestnick is focused on using his position of trust to provide wise counsel to some of the nation's wealthiest families and in so doing help to direct resources in a productive and virtuous way to benefit society and to build God's kingdom on earth.

Just as Solomon shared his wisdom in Proverbs, Cestnick shares a bit of wisdom here.

"As many people become increasingly concerned about the world's fragile social and economic state, I would offer the following perspective: The Bible talks about these types of events. Are we in that era that the Bible refers to as the end times? I'd say so. Certainly from an economic perspective we're seeing things happen that we've never seen before (entire countries on the verge of bankruptcy, for example).

"I believe in being prepared. I don't really worry or concern myself about the timing of the end times too much because I just believe in always being prepared. That means being in a right relationship with God. It means putting my priorities in the right place and making sure my family is well prepared as well. Preparation is critical.

"As the Bible says, he will come like a thief in the night [1 Thessalonians 5:2], in the twinkling of an eye [1 Corinthians 15:52]. I think as long as I am prepared I don't have to worry about the exact timing.

"Isaiah 40:31 has been an important Scripture in my own life: *'But those who wait on the LORD Shall renew their strength; They shall mount up with wings like eagles, They shall run and not be weary, They shall walk and not faint'* [NKJV]. We need to recognize that if our hope is in the Lord, our strength will be renewed. We won't grow faint; we will have the strength to get through."

CHAPTER 22

May You Prosper as Your Soul Prospers

Neleitha Hewitt

"The effective, fervent prayer of a righteous man avails much."

James 5:16 NKJV

I don't expect that there is anyone reading this book who is not looking for a way to improve their financial lot in life, and there is nothing wrong with that. However, we need to grow and prosper spiritually first, and the material things will be added.

It is in this light that I want to tell the story of Pastor Neleitha Hewitt, my colleague and pastor, a Jamaican woman who emigrated from her native country to Canada. Her testimony in this book speaks of achieving financial independence and triumph over adversity and also of purpose towards building God's Kingdom.

"I was raised by parents who were farmers. They had a large banana plantation. My mother worked on the farm with my dad.

"My mother was a praying mother. She always prayed for her children, and while she was helping Dad she would take time out to find a place to pray. It was always the same prayer, derived from Psalm 109: 'Lord, please do not let my children seek their bread out of desolate places.' I do not know if there was more said in this prayer, but that is the part of the prayer I would hear. Whenever I arrived home from school I would go to the farm to see my mother. I could only find her by following her voice while she was praying for her children.

"My mother was illiterate, yet she had an encyclopedic knowledge of the Bible and was very specific about which verses we children were to read aloud to her. My parents had 12 children, and the prayer my mother prayed was answered; not one of us had to seek our bread out of desolate places.

"Another prayer my mother would pray was 'Lord, do not let me die until I see my youngest child pass the worse,' meaning do not let her die until her youngest child is grown up.

"My mother lived to see her youngest child grown and successful. My youngest sibling is a pastor, as I am. Ironically, it was my younger sister who officiated at the service for my mother's funeral, another answered prayer."

Eventually Neleitha and her siblings pursued their dreams and destinies away from Jamaica and came to the United States and Canada.

Neleitha headed north to Toronto in the 1970s. In those days as a black immigrant woman from the islands, it was tough sledding. Her education there was not recognized here. She worked two jobs, as a domestic and a factory worker, and struggled to build a better life.

"I was not satisfied so I then decided that I wanted more out of life, so I returned to school. I attended high school to receive the required credits for college. I then took a data entry course at a local business school in order to get a half-decent job. At that point I was able to care for my family back in Jamaica, and eventually my son joined me here in Canada.

"I then proceeded to Seneca College, where I studied computers. I became a computer operator. After graduation from Seneca College I got a job with People's Jewellers as a data entry operator.

"Later I met my husband, who is now my ex-husband. Our marriage failed because he did not know how to be faithful. I knew he was not someone that I should have married. But I did it regardless. From the time we got married he started to have extramarital affairs, but I tried to hold on because of what my mother had told me. She said, 'Divorce is a disgrace.'

"I felt emptiness in my life, so I started going to church, and eventually I got saved and baptized and became a Christian. Even though I was not happy in my marriage I prayed to God that if it was his will for my life to stay married to let it be so.

"However, my husband decided to leave the marriage two weeks later. He went to the bank and withdrew all our savings, unknown to me. But before he walked out the door he turned and said something to me. He said, 'When I am finished with you, woman, even welfare won't want you!'

"My children and I struggled, but, thank God, I never had to go on welfare. There were times when I did not have enough food to feed my son and my adopted daughter, but I fed them. Once when I went to make dinner for my children I had no rice or money to buy it. I did not say anything to the children. I just went down on my knees and began to pray.

"While I was praying I received a phone call. Someone called to ask if I had any rice. It was bizarre, because at that very moment that's exactly what I was praying for. Probably because of the stress and worry, when the person asked I broke down and started crying. God had provided exactly what I needed and more, because that person brought me rice and additional food, enough to feed me and my children for a week, at a time when, frankly, I had no means to buy food. I realized my mother taught us well.

"I was at the Prayer Palace Church, a large evangelical church in Toronto, and when I knelt down to pray with my hands lifted up, someone came behind me and opened my hands and placed something in them. I turned around and opened my eyes, and it was Pastor Paul Melinchuck, the senior pastor. He placed money in my hands and walked away.

"God has worked many miracles in my life, and he has never left me without comfort. There was another instance where the only money I had was five dollars, and I gave it as an offering in church. On my way home from church I ran out of gas. It was so funny because I ran out of gas in front of a gas station. The attendant came over to me and asked me what was wrong with my car. I said, 'I ran out of gas, and I have no money.' He said, 'I will put gas in, but please return to pay me.' I told him when I would be getting paid and that I would return to pay him, and I did pay him.

"From that point I did not worry about gas. If I needed gas I would return to that same gas station, get gas in advance and pay later. God has made a way for me. I encourage all mothers to pray for their children."

What is clear in Neleitha's testimony is that the Christian law of attraction was working in her favour. She went on to discuss her need for clothing after she discarded the outfits from her worldly life.

"Now as a Christian I was not comfortable with the clothes that I wore previously, because I used to wear them to nightclubs, so I gave them away. I was only left with six suits to wear to work and to church.

"One day I met a designer who lived in the building next door to mine. He saw me going to church, and he told me that he liked the way I was dressed. One day I was praying and I heard a knock at my door. I opened it, and it was the designer. He told me that he was praying and felt the need to design clothes for me for free. He said the Lord would bless him if he began to make clothes for me. From that day onward, every

Saturday he brought me the most beautiful one-of-kind dresses you could ever imagine.

"What I didn't realize at the time was that God was going to use my innate fashion sense and interest in fashion that I had had since I was a young girl growing up in Jamaica as a means to bring provision to raise my family.

"When I became a Christian the Scripture that the Lord gave me was from Ezekiel 16: '*I adorned you with ornaments, put bracelets on your wrists, and a chain on your neck. And I put a jewel in your nose, earrings in your ears, and a beautiful crown on your head. Thus you were adorned with gold and silver, and your clothing was of fine linen, silk, and embroidered cloth*' (Ezekiel 16:11–13 NKJV). Now when I went to church on Sundays I was decked out in these beautiful outfits like those referred to in the passage, and soon the women in the church came flocking to me to find out how they could get these outfits. This resulted in the designer making dresses for many of the church ladies. He went on to become a well-known designer, and indeed the Lord did bless him.

"As I began to see what the Lord was doing; my ambition grew, so I decided that I wanted my own business. I returned to school to take a course in fashion merchandising and sales, which prepared me for starting my own business, which was successful. I became a personal consultant for women's attire. Women would come to my store for me to dress them, which means I picked out their outfits.

"My life was transformed. I was taking trips to New York and Paris to buy fine fashions. I stayed at fine hotels, ate in the best restaurants. I was living the jet-set lifestyle."

Life changed dramatically. She went from being destitute, abandoned and left penniless by her ex-husband to a successful business woman able to own a beautiful home in one of Toronto's finest neighbourhoods and to give her children the kind of life that she once could only have dreamed of.

But later, as Neleitha's life continued to improve, she was put to the ultimate test of her ability to forgive.

"I got to the point where I had forgiven my ex-husband, but that was the word speaking. The true test came for me after a while when my ex-husband's business was not doing well at all and he was going to lose it. He then came to me for a loan, a financial loan, and I gave it to him. This was due to the God in me and the power of forgiveness, which caused me to prosper, and at the same time it freed me. He now tells people that I am the only true Christian he knows."

Eventually, Nellie took another dramatic step, and that was to become a pastor and to work in ministry with Bruce Smith through King Bay Chaplaincy in Sparrow Way, a tough public housing project in Toronto. She continues to minister widely, with a special emphasis on single mothers and young women, and to share her testimony that no matter how bleak things look, God will provide a way for you.

God supernaturally intervenes in the affairs of the righteous to grant them exceptional favour so that they can grow in faith and also to allow them to fulfill the *chazown* that he has laid out for their lives.

CHAPTER 23

The Kingdom of Heaven Is Like Treasure

Philip Phillips

"Again, the kingdom of heaven is like treasure hidden in a field, which a man found and hid; and for joy over it he goes and sells all that he has and buys that field."

Matthew 13:44 NKJV

Although the truth and promise of the kingdom is available for all humanity, unfortunately many do not even know of its existence, not because God has concealed it from them but simply because they haven't been looking for it (*"Seek, and you will find,"* Matthew 7:7 NKJV).

This is underlined in this passage from Matthew's Gospel. In it Christ likens the kingdom to treasure found by a man, who upon finding it immediately hides it to conceal it from others, then sells everything he has to go and to buy that field.

Such was the case for Pastor Philip Phillips, who found his treasure buried in the field in, of all places, an airport.

A native of South India, Pastor Phillips gave his life to the Lord at the age of seven, became a successful businessman, then gave it up to answer the call to become a pastor. Subsequently he moved to Canada to pursue his ministry, but his real purpose was discovered when on a trip to the Toronto airport during the mid-1970s when God told him he wanted him to start a ministry there.

The request was both overwhelming and baffling, and the series of events that followed were both amazing and quite amusing when he tried to make this very unusual heavenly request a reality.

"I said, 'Lord what am I to do?' And then I thought, how can I start it? So, one Friday morning I was praying, and the Lord said, 'I want you to go to the airport and start the work.' I didn't know where to go.

"I went to the airport and parked the car in a public garage and went to security. I asked her, 'Who is the boss here?' She looked at me and said, 'Boss? Sir, they have all kinds of bosses here.' And then I said, 'Suppose I wanted to get permission for something.' 'Oh, you want to talk to the boss of bosses?' And then I thought, boss of bosses? She might mean one of these Mafia groups, boss of bosses.

"Then the security woman said, 'You have to go to that building in the open field, that four-storey building. That is the boss of bosses in there. He's a general manager.' So, I walked across that field and went to the building, and then I stood before the elevator, and somebody said, 'He's on the second floor.'

"I got in and pressed the number two, and it opened at the general manager's office. I went in, and one of the receptionists said, 'What do you want?' I said, 'I'd like to see the general manager.' 'Oh, do you have an appointment?' I said, 'No, ma'am, I have no appointment.' 'No, sir, you cannot simply go in and see him. He is a very busy man.' 'Can I make an appointment?' 'Oh, sure you can. It may take about two weeks.' I said, 'That's fine. I'll wait until then.' 'OK. What's your name?' I said, 'My name is Reverend Phillips.' 'Oh, you are a reverend? In that case, I can squeeze you in between two appointments.'

"I waited there, and then one of them called me and said, 'Come in.' So, I went in. The boss is a big boss. He never even looked at me. He looked down and was signing something. Without looking at me he said, 'What can I do for you?' I said, 'Sir, I'd like to make an appointment with you.' 'For what?' I said, 'I'd like to talk about something very important.' 'What is that?' 'I want to start an office for a chaplain.' 'Chaplain? We have nothing to do with the chaplains here. We are very busy people,' and so on.

"'But the Lord told me to come and ask you.' 'What?' He was so surprised. 'Even God told you?' 'Yeah.'

"Suddenly he found time. He said, 'I have nothing to do with God and the business, but did you say that God told you?' I said, 'That's what I felt.' 'Do you do this kind of work here, sir?' he asked. I told him that I was a national chaplain of the armed forces of India, and now the Lord had brought me here.

"So he called his secretary and the building manager, and he said, 'This gentleman wants to start something. He said God told him. I don't know. But please take him and explain to him.'

"So they gave me about a half-hour lecture so that I would never come back again. They discouraged me in every way possible, but one gentleman was told, 'Because he talked about God, just take his full information, in case God does something; then we will have to listen.'

"So I went back, and I started praying. I said, 'Lord, you told me to go there. Please let me know.' And six months later I had the first call. 'Reverend Philips, you're the one who came and talked about chaplains. We don't have any guarantee, but recently there's been a development here. We had to open a first aid clinic, but now we don't need it, so we have this place available, and if you'd like we can talk about it."

So after about six months of negotiations with the Airport Authority and bringing all of the major Christian denominations on board, Phillips had his ministry in the airport, which then expanded across Canada to nine major airports. He headed it up for over 30 years until stepping down recently.

When Pastor Phillips was told by God to start a ministry at the airport, he had no idea where to start, where to go or who to talk to. When he did find the people to talk to, they politely told him to get lost, but he wasn't dismayed. He kept praying, and God not only answered his prayer, he gave him a huge nationwide chaplaincy, ministering to Canadians from coast to coast.

The point is that God's kingdom has a treasure planted in a field somewhere for all of us. All we need to do through the transition is to seek, trust and obey to discover it.

Chapter 24

The Kingdom Promise, Summary

"Then shall the King say unto them on His right hand, Come, ye blessed of my Father, inherit the kingdom prepared for you from the foundation of the world."

Matthew 25:34 KJV

This book has been written as an initial installment in Gary Gradley's *Trusting Through the Transition* series to give us a deeper and more profound understanding of kingdom principles so that we are fortified and strengthened as challenges are presented to us.

The Keys to the Kingdom

The Promises of God: The promises of God are irrevocable and cannot return void, and we who are Christians are heirs to God's promise of blessing to the descendants of Abraham, through the blood of Jesus.

There Is a God, and It Ain't You: All of us need to acknowledge God as the creator of the universe and everything in it, including all of us. We need to realize that we are made for God; God is not made for us.

Seek Ye First the Kingdom: The world is based on pursuing your earthly needs first and then working your way up to higher consciousness after this has been accomplished. The kingdom turns this paradigm upside down and tells you to pursue God and his righteousness first and then your earthly needs will be added unto you.

The Kingdom of God: The kingdom is a place that we can't truly comprehend in our earthly realm, a place laid up for the righteous to spend eternity with Jesus and God. We should not sacrifice this reward for short-term earthly riches but should sacrifice if necessary earthly treasures for a 100-fold payback in this life and the next in the kingdom.

The Kingdom of Canada: Canadian Christians have a duty and responsibility to not only strengthen their own faith but work for the communal good of the entire nation to fulfill the purpose of Canada as a kingdom country.

Kingdom Culture and Citizenship: People who are citizens and followers of the kingdom are different than those who are of the world; they have different values, goals and standards. They do not conform to the ways of this world and are not seduced by human wisdom and desires.

The Bible: Study the Word of God; it is your own personal operational manual.

Faith over Fear: That overwhelming emotion of fear that's haunting you is not from God. We need to learn to trust in God and his sovereignty over our lives so we can triumph and achieve our purpose.

Chazown: Chazown or vision is what God gives us to reveal the purpose for our lives. Too many of us pursue worldly goals before seeking him, run ahead of God and create our own vision for our lives and then bring it to him to get him to affirm it. However, our plans are those of the flesh; thus they are flawed. God's plan for us is perfect, because it reveals our true purpose on earth, and he will provide the resources that we need to accomplish it.

Trust in God, 100 Per cent: God *is* worthy of 100 per cent of your trust. Nothing else in the world is. So lean on God and trust God more and more each day.

Leap of Faith: In the kingdom we must live by faith, not by sight, and at some point we will have to take a bold step to believe in God to accomplish our purpose in life.

The Power of Prayer: Prayer is the power source that fuels the Kingdom Promise. We need to go to God in humility and praise and put our needs in front of him. If we don't ask, we won't receive. The Lord's Prayer is the perfect prayer, which every believer should pray daily to ensure a productive prayer life.

"I Am the Vine": We need to see ourselves as branches connected to the vine, Jesus. Without the vine we are powerless and we will not produce any fruit.

Seventy Times Seven: Unforgiveness not only can destroy our health but separates us from God. Learning to forgive is essential for a successful life.

Sowing and Reaping: As well as prayer, repentance and forgiveness, we need to pay our tithes and offerings to God so we can avail ourselves of the treasures God has in store for us.

The Wisdom of Solomon: The principles of Solomon's Proverbs represent eternal godly wisdom to guide and direct us in our lives.

Prosper as Your Soul Prospers: God will provide for his followers and provide the favour, people and resources that they need to be successful.

The Kingdom of Heaven Is Like Treasure: This is an amazing eternal secret that has been revealed to you. Like the man in Christ's parable, protect that treasure and then take everything you have and trade it for the treasure.

What is amazing about the Kingdom Promise is how simple it is. Christ gave us two simple instructions, to seek the kingdom and his righteousness, and everything we desire in this world and the next will be ours. That's probably why so many people don't get it, because we are all looking for some complicated, difficult formula that only the brightest, most educated and richest can access.

The key is to not fall prey to the ways of the world and miss the Kingdom Promise. Don't forget that the ways of God are not the ways of man and will manifest in a different manner: *"For my thoughts are not your thoughts, neither are your ways my ways, saith the LORD. For as the heavens are higher than the earth, so are my ways higher than your ways, and my thoughts than your thoughts"* (Isaiah 55:8–9 KJV). This excerpt from Isaiah in the Old Testament reinforces the theme, which speaks to the consistency and timelessness of the kingdom concept.

Finally, make today the day when you seize hold of both your earthly and eternal destiny and surrender your will to the will of God so that you can experience the greatness that he has laid up for you.

The kingdom has been built like the universe and the earth by God for those who follow him and believe in his eternal promises. He has given us a road map, which we need to use every day to prevail.

In closing, let us go back to Gary's original purpose for the book, which was to instruct people dealing with crises to turn back to God to cope. The point was outlined by Jesus in Matthew 7:

> *Therefore whoever hears these sayings of Mine, and does them, I will liken him to a wise man who built his house on the rock: and the rain descended, the floods came, and the winds blew and beat on that house; and it did not fall, for it was founded on the rock. But everyone who hears these sayings of Mine, and does not do them, will be like a foolish*

man who built his house on the sand: and the rain descended, the floods came, and the winds blew and beat on that house; and it fell. And great was its fall. (Matthew 7:24–27 NKJV)

Faith in Action

Move into Action with Application Action Planning

Congratulations on getting here! Hopefully you have been inspired and moved by what you have read. Perhaps you have some idea of what you would like to take and apply, believing that it will bring value to you, others and the kingdom of God.

This section is intended to inspire you to commit to taking action in applying what you have been reading. Nothing will really change unless you do something different. Daily application is what will make a difference in transforming your life.

If you want to

- Continue to build your faith, hope and trust in God and in life
- Feel closer and more in tune with God, Jesus and the Holy Spirit
- Hear God's divine will and guidance more clearly and be obedient, taking action on it
- Be at peace regardless of the challenging reality around you
- Better manage your self-talk and affirm a positive future
- Stay connected with other believers
- Build and expand the kingdom of God

then this Application Action Planning section will be very important and valuable to you.

The Kingdom Promise

1) First decide what you would like to accomplish as an outcome from a committed daily practice of devotion. Pray about it as well.

Record now what that is for you:

_____

_____

_____

_____

_____

2) Next, to ensure achievement of your written objective, decide what aspects of your faith you would like to develop. Pray about it as well. Here are some examples:

Keep a deep daily devotion and self-care routine.
Pray daily and be in the Word daily.
Attend church and hear the Word preached.
Gather godly evidence.
Practice positive self-talk and affirmation.
Be in relationship with and accountable to other believers.
Know that God loves me.

Record now what that is for you:

_____

_____

_____

_____

_____

3) Now read each of the sections, following step 5, which gives you some valuable suggestions on how to grow in that area of building your faith. As you read make notes about what you would like to apply:

_____

_____

_____

_____

_____

_____

4) Make a commitment to God, yourself and others as to what specifically you will do daily and weekly:

_____

_____

_____

_____

_____

_____

5) Support and accountability are critical. Decide who you will work with as a support and accountability partner, a spouse, friend, associate, etc., most likely a believer, who you will make your commit to. Ideally you and your partner should talk and support each other weekly in staying on track with what you committed to doing. This is very powerful and will enable you to create new habits that rapidly grow your faith.

How to Build Your Faith

Reread and study the proven faith-based principles and practices in this book and consider attending our webinars and workshops to rapidly build and maintain your faith.

Learn and apply the following strategies and practices to strengthen yourself mentally, emotionally, physically, financially and spiritually.

Have a daily devotion and self-care routine: Invest daily in your relationship with God, Jesus and the Holy Spirit. Dr. David Mainse, Pastor John Arnott, Bruxy Cavey, Lorna Dueck, Paul Henderson, Tim Cestnick and more all said that the foundation of their success was having a deep personal intimate relationship with God, daily reading God's Word, praying deeply, hearing God's will for them and obeying God.

Pray Daily

Prayer is the currency of the kingdom.

Prayer is us talking to God, Jesus and the Holy Spirit and receiving their divine will and guidance.

Prayer puts us in communication with the Almighty and deepens our relationship with the Divine. Prayer demonstrates our dependence and often our surrender to God's will.

The Kingdom Promise

The deeper we are in relationship with God, the more God acts, guides and provides in our lives.

I use and recommend the ACTS formula for powerful praying:

Adoration: Acknowledge God and his sovereignty.
Confession: Confess your sins and shortcomings.
Thanksgiving: Thank God for all the things that you are grateful for.
Supplication: Ask for all the things that you desire.

Be deeply grateful every day, and give God the praise and glory for providing (not yourself for doing it). Be filled with deep emotional gratitude from your heart. God feels and enjoys it and will bless you even more when you give the praise, glory, honour and gratitude back to him.

Ask to be filled with the Holy Spirit, with the spirit and presence of the true Lord Jesus Christ of Nazareth, who was born in the flesh and died on the cross to pay for our sins because of God's love for us. God does answer our prayers when we ask properly.

Ask God to speak to you and guide you in your life and in your next steps and decisions. Ask God first for his will and perfect guidance, especially when making important decisions.

Be in the Word Daily

Reading the Bible regularly will build your faith because:

- God speaks to us through His Word and reveals his character, love and promises to us.
- It provides overwhelming evidence that God is faithful, works miracles and does provide.
- It teaches us God's kingdom principles by which we should live to have the fullest life and to serve God.
- It gives us many good examples of walking rightly with God and the best example of Jesus Christ to model our character after.
- It shows us how to love and be love-based servant leaders.

Suggested Practice

Follow a reading schedule as suggested in many "read the Bible in a year" programs.

Read specific Scriptures for specific reasons, e.g., Proverbs for wisdom, The New Testament Gospels for the teachings of Jesus.

Recommended Process When Reading the Bible:

- Read it in context.
- Meditate on it.
- Become convicted of a certain Scripture.
- Memorize it.
- Learn and understand it.
- Live it.

Gather Godly Evidence

- Deliberately look for and gather evidence, proof of the power of faith, the power of prayer, the power of God, proof that God does provide.
- Reread parts of this book again to fully and deeply connect to and believe the stories of faith as overwhelming evidence of the power of God and the power of faith.
- Study, read or listen to all of God's promises that are throughout the Bible.
- Go to our website, www.TrustingThroughTheTransition.com, to conveniently download all of these promises of God.
- God cannot break his Word—his promises. These promises are for you as righteous believer. Read them daily or record them and listen to them daily, internalize them and believe that these promises are for you, that you are a beloved child of God, worthy and deserving of all of God's promises, gifts, miracles, abundance and love.

You will want to develop your faith in God, the Creator, that everything is unfolding perfectly as per God's perfect and divine plan, even though your mind sees and thinks otherwise.

God and your faith is the only real solution!

We must learn to focus on God and shift our attention from fear to faith because God is bigger than all our problems.

If you are in a place of despair and hopelessness, you can experience a miracle and break out of that mental, emotional prison.

Positive Self-Talk and Affirmation

Develop your ability to manage and control your self-talk and choose faith over fear each and every moment. In other words, develop and strengthen your resiliency.

The more that you can practice and maintain the mental, emotional and spiritual state of acceptance, peace and love, the more you will walk through the chaos relatively unscathed.

I believe that our strong faith truly can deliver us from experiencing severe financial hardships.

Mastering your self-talk and staying focused on the positive, staying in faith, is absolutely critical when going through challenging times. Remember, what we constantly think about expands and attracts more of the same into our lives. That's the law of attraction!

The key is to fill your mind daily with good thoughts, good information and good images. The best of these good thoughts are about God, Jesus, and the Holy Spirit. Memorize empowering Scripture passages and play them in your mind daily. Be in the Word daily.

Perhaps you would find value in a daily affirmation that strengthens your faith. Here are two examples:

I believe in God, Jesus and the Holy Spirit, the purest, highest energy, which is love.

I believe in God's divine plan for me.

I believe that God loves me, protects me and provides for me unconditionally.

I choose unconditional love, which gives me freedom and joy.

I trust in God, which gives me peace.

I choose only positive loving thoughts.

I believe in the power of faith and belief.

I believe in the power of prayer.

And I believe in the bliss of gratitude through the Holy Spirit.

Entrepreneurs Psalm 23
By Thomas Henshell

1. The Lord is my leader and largest shareholder,
   He has provided all that I need.
2. He forces me to stop talking, be quiet, and sit in calm places,
   he takes time out to mentor me.
3. He encourages and refreshes my soul.
   He tells me the right things to do
   for his glory, not my own.
4. When it feels like I walk every hour of every day
   In the valley of difficulty

I will not fear I am wasting my time and talent
nor am I alone,
for you are with me;
Your family and your influence
they comfort me.
5. You prepare a feast for me in the presence
of my naysayers and critics,
You put "superstar" on my business card
my confidence overflows.
Your goodness and love go with me
In every meeting,
in every phone call,
and in every email.
And I will work for the Lord and Associates forever.

Be in Relationship with Other Believers

As Bruxy Cavey shared in chapter 12, "Blindsided," it was the power of other Christians supporting, encouraging and loving him that restored him from identity loss and depression to being a fully functional human being once again.

There is strength in numbers, and teamwork works.

Pray for each other. Ask for prayer when needed. Don't be shy or embarrassed; ask for God's help through the encouragement, support and prayers of others.

Personally, I have received a number of mini-miracles through the prayers of other believers. They continue to be a real encouragement and blessing for me, especially in times of need.

So invest time, energy and love into building these valuable life-giving relationships. Give and serve first, and you will receive the same.

Know that God Loves You

As you read, meditate on the Word, pray and practice these kingdom principles, recognize and know that God truly does love you intimately and unconditionally. You are one of God's creations, and God loves, protects and provides for his own creation—you.

Progressively deepen your faith by trusting in God for the "little things." When God is faithful with these, trust and risk more for bigger things.

Summary

Your daily devotion practice is critical to you surviving and thriving mentally, emotionally, physically, financially and spiritually. When you do it consistently, daily, it will transform your life, just as Philippians 4:4–7 promises:

> *Rejoice in the Lord always. Again I will say, rejoice! Let your gentleness be known to all men. The Lord is at hand. Be anxious for nothing, but in everything by prayer and supplication, with thanksgiving, let your requests be made known to God; and the peace of God, which surpasses all understanding, will guard your hearts and minds through Christ Jesus.* (NKJV)

May you walk closely in faith with God, and may your life be a real blessing to others and to God.

May God bless you as you continue to do his will.

For his purpose and glory!

Blessings on your journey, with love.

Trusting Through the Transition Resources and Services

Products and Services:

A range of engaging and interactive products and services that support the acute spiritual, financial and practical daily living needs of people living amidst spiritual and social-economic change and chaos.

An integrated multi-platform, full service/one stop range of products and services, including: books, visual reminders, audio and DVD products, live seminars, workshops/webinars, coaching services, support groups, websites, network of resources, charitable opportunities and more.

To learn more about our products and services, including speaking at your gathering, please call us at (416) 219-2943 or email: info@TrustingThroughTheTransition.com or visit our websites, *www.TrustingThroughTheTransition.com* and *www.KingdomPromise.com*

The next book in the series is *Conquering the Social Economic Storm: Your Practical Personal and Financial Survival Guide to Thriving through the Transition.*

This book and workshop combine and integrate the important elements of spiritual, mental and emotional practices with sound financial principles and practices to prepare you and your family to survive and thrive through the transition.

Once again I will be interviewing many leading spiritual, personal development and financial experts, sharing their knowledge and recommendations for your immediate benefit.

The valuable content will include:

- How to consistently choose to be in a state of love and faith that provides divine guidance, protection and provision.
- How to be prepared emotionally and physically for the potentially life-altering impact of a social-economic crisis.
- How to rapidly change your spending habits and start living within your financial means.
- How to sell off assets early to aggressively pay off debt, since crushing debt will be a killer.
- Many daily living and financial practices to take action on that will ensure your family's safety and well-being.
- How to know God's purpose for your life and start living on purpose and being a leader through the transition.
- And much more.

Phil Kershaw

Phil Kershaw is a veteran business executive with extensive experience in the communications, sports and political arenas. Kershaw has headed up his own successful advertising agency for 16 years, was a three-time President of the Saskatchewan Roughriders, Chairman and interim commissioner of the Canadian Football League, President of the Ottawa Rough Riders and served as a consultant for the Ottawa Renegades. He was twice appointed by the Prime Minister including as a Director of Canada 125 in 1992.

Gary Gradley

For the last 20 years Gary Gradley has run a very successful national training and development business and a personal development coaching business, working with over 20,000 leaders, employees, and individuals throughout Canada, USA and Australia. He spent 6 years facilitating various high-profile personal development seminars. He is a trusted advisor for many national corporations throughout Ontario.

CASTLE QUAY BOOKS